HE SETS THE PRISONER FREE

A NEW CREATION in Jail but Still a CAPTIVE in My Mind

SHAWN HURLEY

KAINOS PUBLISHING

An imprint of:
SUPERNATURAL TRUTH PRODUCTIONS, LLC
Practical Training for Spirit-Filled Living
www.SupernaturalTruth.com

Copyright © 2023, Shawn Hurley

All rights reserved. This book is protected by the copyright laws of the United States of America. No portion of this work may be copied or reprinted for commercial gain or mass distribution or profit. No part of this book may be reproduced or used in any manner without the prior written permission of the copyright owner, except for the use of brief quotations in a book review. The use of short quotations or the copying of an occasional page for personal or group study is permitted and encouraged. Permission will be granted upon request. For permission, contact the publisher through its web site at SupernaturalTruth.com.

Unless otherwise indicated, all Scripture quotations are taken from the Holy Bible, New International Version®, NIV®. Copyright © 1973, 1978, 1984, 2011 by Biblica, Inc.™ Used by permission of Zondervan. All rights reserved worldwide. www.zondervan.com The "NIV" and "New International Version" are trademarks registered in the United States Patent and Trademark Office by Biblica, Inc.™

All Scripture quotations marked (NKJV) are taken from the New King James Version®. Copyright © 1982 by Thomas Nelson. Used by permission. All rights reserved.

MATURE CONTENT: This book includes true stories of the author's life. As such, there are very mature themes that readers should be aware of, including child neglect, child abuse, suicidal thoughts, alcoholism, drug abuse, abortion, incarceration, and mentions of sexual activity. The goal is not to glorify sin but Jesus who liberates. Nevertheless, harsh details are shared to give hope to those personally experiencing or ministering to others in similar circumstances. Readers should be aware of this and proceed accordingly.

ISBN: 978-1-959547-04-4

"Theology is knowing what God would do. Love is doing it." Shawn Hurley said that, and it's had a profound impact on me ever since. As his longtime friend, I can say in good conscience that this book is but a reflection of the extravagant love Shawn regularly exhibits in both his public and private life. I believe it will inspire you to better know God's healing love and reciprocate it to others in miraculous ways.

Josh Adkins
Founder of Loft Church, Author, and Speaker
JoshAdkins.org

Shawn Hurley's humility and love have always been an inspiration to me. He has a true ministry of healing that reminds me of Smith Wigglesworth, and he carries himself with the humility of a man who knows he stands by grace. His story will not only inspire you; it will drive you to worship the Lord, our Redeemer.

With simplicity and candor, Shawn will convince you that absolutely no one, including you, is disqualified from being loved by God and being used to bring him glory. Don't just read this book to hear amazing stories; let Shawn's journey and teaching lead you into your own encounter with the God who sets prisoners free.

JonMark Baker
Evangelist and Author
JonMarkBaker.com

I don't know anyone who has sacrificed more time to minister healing and the gospel than Shawn Hurley. And that's probably why he has witnessed more miracles than most Christians. How does someone dedicate so much time and attention to ministry? It's easy. For Shawn, it's not technically "ministry;" it's just the overflow of who he is in Christ. It's natural.

As you read Shawn's stories and some of the revelations that have shaped his life, let the Holy Spirit produce the same grace in your life. Let this book be a launchpad into a deeper relationship with God and a greater expression of the new creation.

Art Thomas
Missionary-Evangelist and Founder of Roots Church
ArtThomas.org

CONTENTS

Acknowledgments   7
Preface   9

Section 1: My Story

Chapter 1:   A Baptism of Fire   15
Chapter 2:   From Darkness to Light   41
Chapter 3:   Saved as a Son   71

Section 2: Our Story

Chapter 4:   A New Creation   91
Chapter 5:   Love Never Fails   99
Chapter 6:   The Vine and the Branches   105
Chapter 7:   Greater Works than These   117
Chapter 8:   Walking in Power   123

Afterword   129

About the Author   131

HE SETS THE PRISONER FREE ~ SHAWN HURLEY

ACKNOWLEDGMENTS

I would like to thank my boys for walking through my personal trials and for forgiving me for my failings as a father. I would also like to thank my wife for her faithful love, support, and companionship in good times and bad. Finally, I wish to acknowledge my friend Mark Dooley, whom the Holy Spirit brought into my life to make this book possible.

PREFACE

Today, I am a man transformed by the power of God. I travel the world praying for the sick and seeing them miraculously cured. I have laid hands on thousands of people and watched their diseases simply melt away. And to those suffering from anguish, despair, or a broken heart, I bring a message of redeeming hope that salvation is available for all. In most cases, their demons flee, and their shattered lives are restored to peace and harmony. In all this, I depend solely on divine supply, never asking for a cent to do what I have been commanded by Christ: "Heal the sick, raise the dead, cleanse those who have leprosy, drive out demons. Freely you have received; freely give" (Matthew 10:8). Those are the words I now live by, after putting my total trust in a God who, I have learned, loves me deeply.

I live for God and am moved by him, and he rescued me from the pit. That is because I was not always the man I am now. Indeed, for most of my life, I lived as though God did not exist. I was a deeply troubled child, a tormented teen, a convict, an addict, and someone bent on destruction. I was homeless and forced to eat from trash cans. I was disloyal, untrustworthy, and saw everyone as a threat rather than a source of solace or love. In short,

HE SETS THE PRISONER FREE ~ SHAWN HURLEY

I was as far from the kingdom of God as you could get, content to dwell in a realm of darkness and decay. My hands were more used to fighting than praying, and if you had told me that one day, I would see miracles performed through those hands, I probably would have struck you.

But that is exactly what happened: I discovered, even amid that terrible darkness, that I was and am loved by the Creator. I was loved then just as I am loved now. What's more, I am loved as his *child*. Discovering that we are all children of the living God was the greatest revelation of my life. It proved to me that if we are of God, then we must surely be capable of a godly and supernatural existence. We can indeed heal the sick, raise the dead, and cleanse the lepers. We can cast out demons and command all things that are not of God to bow before his Word. Once I accepted my divine sonship, I proved the truth of this amazing reality for myself.

This is the story of how I was led from darkness into light. It is the story of salvation as my blind eyes were opened to the wonder of my Father's love. And in that love, I found redemption from the worst of sins and was given the power to heal, help, and deliver. In sharing this, my hope is that the readers of this book will discover that no life or situation is beyond God's love. As his child, you, too, can become one with him so that miracles will then become the norm. I was broken, bruised, and debased, but he raised me up to see my true potential and value as someone made in his image and likeness. I was dead, but now I am alive, thanks to

PREFACE

a love that makes all things new. Such is your birthright, and my aim in this book is to help you realize this incredible reality.

HE SETS THE PRISONER FREE ~ SHAWN HURLEY

PART 1
MY STORY

Chapter 1

A Baptism of Fire

You can have hope. No matter how dark and devastating your past, Jesus is greater. No matter how evil your enemy is, the gospel can reach them. No matter how broken that person in your life is, God can make them whole.

I'm proof.

God doesn't make mistakes. Anyone could have looked at my life growing up and thought God finally messed up, but today my history has become a signpost for you, pointing to the God who does the impossible. This is a story of one man. It is a true story and, hopefully, one that will make you think about your own life with its accomplishments and failings. It is also a story of God's love—his patient love for one man. And since he is no respecter of men, this same patience and mercy applies to all, including you.

When a child is born, we know that the parents can have their own challenging issues at times concerning nurturing and other parenting skills. We can see that even though there are

HE SETS THE PRISONER FREE ~ SHAWN HURLEY

different variables when it comes to parenting, all environments, whether good or difficult, can produce children who become successful and well-rounded. But two variables seem to be the greatest common factor when it comes to success or failure: speech and safety within the home.

Unfortunately, I had neither of these in any way. I was born to parents who suffered greatly with degraded personality traits, focusing on their own personal pleasure and masochism and demanding complete obedience through physical pain and even threats of death.

As a child, I had no liberty to speak or think outside their fears or delusions. By the age of six, I was filled with every fear and warped sense of behavior imaginable for a child who lived in this type of environment. Today, I would be diagnosed with ADHD (LMNOPQRST) and all the letters we use to label our children. I had every single label that one could have from school, psychologists, psychiatrists, you name it. But at that time, they labeled a child like me as stubborn. The cure was what they called discipline, but in reality, it was punishment.

I was integrated into the public school system at age six. Fear overwhelmed me. Once in the classroom, all of my senses were heightened and constantly alert for pain and even death to find me. I was ultra-sensitive, identifying quickly who was for me or who was a threat, always anticipating danger that would end my life, making judgments and values about people who would cause me pain. I was constantly in defense mode. I tried to manipulate or

A BAPTISM OF FIRE

outright defy every person in authority because I didn't have the courage to do it at home.

I was stripped of my voice inside the four walls of our apartment, and any expression of my opinion in any way different from my mother's or her boyfriends would most certainly have dire consequences. Nearly all my thoughts were consumed with trying to keep my mother from taking out her anger on me. So I had to be submissive to her in every way.

By the age of seven, I could read every adult's facial expression and anticipate the direction of their conversation so that I could become everything they needed me to be. I was in self-preservation mode and intensely afraid of dying every day.

After continual behavioral problems, I was taken out of public schools at age eight, and my mom enrolled me in Catholic schools run by the French Catholic nuns, God's supposed representatives. Unfortunately, they believed that the quickest way to cure bad behavior was to beat me consistently. They said that this school was run under the guidance of God. I quickly found out they used the same tactics the adults did in my home with one exception. I was told God was this Supreme Being who ran the world, who would sort out the bad kids from the good. (Guess which kind I was.) The good kids would go to a place called heaven where everything was wonderful, and the bad ones would burn in a fire forever and be tortured every day and night. God's supposed representatives would tell me that I was going to burn forever.

HE SETS THE PRISONER FREE ~ SHAWN HURLEY

I could imagine what that was like. My mother would hold my hands over the gas burners. Fire was the most painful thing that I knew of at that age. She would beat me every other day.

I became terrified of this God, but at seven years old, I was pretty smart, and one day, it occurred to me that I knew where God lived: in that huge, dark building called the church. He wore black and gave out round things, and his other name was the priest. I said to myself, *If I burn down this place where God lives, he will die, and I won't burn in this place called hell.* So one day, I stole some matches and ran up to the altar and stared a fire. Unfortunately, God was awake and chased me, but he had to stop to put out the fire, and I got away. Apparently, God didn't recognize me, because I never got in trouble for it. But now I was certain that I would burn forever.

At this time, what little children call the boogeyman started to attack me. Day and night, this demon kicked doors open and physically tortured me. I was now even trying to harm my little brother because of the positive attention he was getting. I was growing worse inside, and the fear of dying never stopped, but it also began to look attractive. I was so lost inside. This boogeyman seemed so real, but no one would listen to me because I had already been a liar for years. I didn't really know about suicide, but I was always thinking about dying. I had a limited and vague understanding of it, but it meant that I wouldn't have to be here anymore. That was all I needed to know. If I could just skip the

A BAPTISM OF FIRE

burning part of this thing called hell, it might have been more appealing.

While all these things were taking place, I did the unthinkable: I tried to end my little brother's life. He was mom's favorite, and only he received her love and affection. As he grew and was lavished with praise and adoration, it was apparent to me that he must go. One day, something whispered in my mind that if I emptied tin cans and placed the sharp lids around him in his crib, he would roll around and cut himself. Thankfully, my mother found them before he woke up. I just wanted to be loved too. I was severely beaten for trying to hurt my little brother.

I was experiencing demonic open visions, and my behavior became more violent and unpredictable. I was smashing objects. I began running away, lying more, and started stealing, and I was only eight years old. Finally, the symptoms of my abuse had manifested in such a way that the authorities stepped in, and I was removed from my home. It was an act of mercy that I was removed from this awful environment, only to be sent another. I was put into an orphanage run by God's representatives, the nuns, and every pedophile and pervert that was not fit for society happened to be employed there.

A casually dressed man showed up one day in the summer of 1970. He was friendly enough and unassuming. Unknown to me until that very moment, my mother had already packed my bag. He said, "I'm going to take you to your new home." It didn't even

HE SETS THE PRISONER FREE ~ SHAWN HURLEY

register with me. My only feelings were of fear and anger and how I could manage those emotions.

There were six cottages in all: four for the boys and two for the girls. I arrived at cottage number four. Kids of all ages were playing some sort of game in the front yard. This Catholic institution was run by French and Irish nuns with secular strongarms (called childcare workers) to keep order and enforce discipline.

Even though I'm about to describe some of the horror that took place, if it weren't for the bits and pieces of right behavior and the greater covering of overall morality of one person, I would have truly become a sociopath. I was already devoid of any empathy, pity, or concern for anyone. Part of the mission statement of the orphanage was to teach young boys and girls how to live a moral, God-fearing life. The only problem was the religious order of the day was using medieval traditions. In other words, they were trying to beat the devil out of you and beat good behavior into you. Behavior modification by placing outward restrictions on the flesh to instill internal morals and values never works in the long term.

Catholicism, the Mass, Jesus, and Me

At eight years old, I was learning Catholic doctrine. Unfortunately, my teachers were carnal. They knew nothing about God but plenty about a religious life. In the mind of an eight-year-old, God looked like the following.

A BAPTISM OF FIRE

I woke up hungry on Sunday mornings. But I was told I couldn't eat until after Mass so I could receive the body of Jesus. Then, I went to a building where I had to sit, stand, kneel, sit, stand, and kneel. Then I had to listen to a man say a bunch of stuff for over an hour. Trying to get a room full of disturbed young boys and girls to be quiet and orderly during Mass was like trying to break into Fort Knox—impossible.

After Mass, we would reap the consequences of our disobedient behavior by sitting in a hard chair for an hour or two without moving or talking. Yes, I was still hungry. Needless to say, God was not appealing at all, especially after being beaten and the many other things done in his name. I thought he was a cruel taskmaster.

Removal from a home environment of psychological, sexual, and corporal abuse is a blessing, and you learn how to go about your daily life as you get older, tucking those scars neatly away. Your mind is focused on self-preservation, and I always did my best to carry on by burying what I had endured.

Later, we learned that in the late sixties and early seventies, large institutions of young boys and girls unfortunately attracted some of the most deviant sexual predators on the planet, both from secular society and religious orders. Coupled with the fact that the older boys had already submitted to former predators and learned to copy their behaviors, sexual abuse was now part of my daily environment.

HE SETS THE PRISONER FREE ~ SHAWN HURLEY

As children, we can survive some injuries with temporary or minimal scars: falls from trees, people constantly yelling at us, even our failures and discipline. We are born with a deep capacity to cope, something like a giant well, so that the things done to a child can be stored, processed, and forgiven.

Other abuse is so heinous that we try to completely block it out and cover the well with a lid that says Do Not Ever Open. But these incidents will still have power over our lives until we take the lid off and clean out the well. Before you do this, you must understand inside yourself that no matter what you find or see, you were a helpless child. You had absolutely no power to stop any of it, and none of what happened was your fault.

I don't have to go into detail about the fear of being alone with grown men and women and older boys and girls, submitting to their most disgusting perversions. This produced shame, guilt, and anger. I was never free to be a child. I never felt as if I belonged anywhere and had no comfort or peace in my own skin. I was among the walking dead. Two new emotions started to gain dominance in me: hate and revenge. I stared to view men and women as the enemy, taking what they wanted and not caring about my feelings or protests, satisfying themselves through my body of flesh, then quickly leaving until the next time.

I couldn't function in any school or social setting. I was always fighting or cursing and had so many other behavioral issues. In kindergarten and first grade, I had punched teachers, nuns, and other kids. They finally had to homeschool me at the orphanage.

A BAPTISM OF FIRE

In all this horror was a ray of sunshine and love that kept me going and saved me from completely giving up. Her name was Sister Marie Clemens. She has been deceased for some time now; I still visit her grave every so often. She is the one who really kept me from imploding and kept me from becoming a complete sociopath. Although devoted to daily religious life, she loved me, she took time with me, she taught me about life, and she took me to Cape Cod on vacations with her and her family.

She took the time to teach me social skills and never hurt me. One person who cared—just one—kept me from what I believe was a life destined to be behind bars forever. I had a list of people I wanted dead, and if I couldn't kill them, then I certainly would kill anyone who resembled them.

Her intercession of loving kindness tempered the hatred inside me and drew a complete moral line in me, as fragile as it was. It showed me that not everyone was bad or deserved to die. I stayed in this horrible situation for two years, and then the monster that these two former environments and the people within had created was released back into society by way of a foster home. I was to be the first child in this new experimental program. They had no idea what they were getting.

The first night, they actually had a candlelit dinner. They were kind and even gave me permission to call them Mom and Dad. As a manipulative, fearful, untrusting soul, I played on every one of their emotions. I made sure their desires and hopes were all

HE SETS THE PRISONER FREE ~ SHAWN HURLEY

fulfilled, making them believe that they were making a difference in the world by taking me into their lives.

I was changing inside, and my thoughts were becoming more curious in nature, wanting to be expressed in the strangest of behaviors. I was obsessed with seeing older women naked and watching things burn. I hung out with teenage girls, hoping for glimpses of them naked and hoping they would engage with me sexually. Secretly, these things were happening because most of the girls I hung out with were messed up also.

At this time, I was wetting the bed almost daily, and the nice new parents were starting to figure out that even though I could be cute at times and give many of the right answers, something was seriously wrong with me.

After school one day, my secret life began to unravel. The police began investigating the increasing numbers of fires and thefts. They had received my name from someone in the neighborhood. The detectives were waiting to question me, but because they had no evidence, I was able to distract them and lied convincingly enough that they left.

The only problem was the evidence of all the stolen paint from the paint factory that was sitting in our garage, and I had already lied to my foster parents about where it came from. They never said a word because there was already opposition to a foster home in the neighborhood.

I was only in third grade and already could barely control my erratic emotions. I was such an angry person inside, and it was

A BAPTISM OF FIRE

starting to exert its two most intense wants: to satisfy my anger through violent actions and to find a woman to love me. In third grade, that meant something that resembled abuse, just like at the orphanage.

My foster parents requested psychiatric help for me after it was discovered that I was lighting hairspray cans on fire so they would act like flame throwers. The placement agency assigned a psychiatrist to me.

I was a child in stature and age with basic intelligence, but I had another skill, one that I learned from being brought up in an environment of fear and abuse: survival. Internally, I was mature beyond my years and could read every face and figure out the direction of every conversation. I trusted absolutely no one except my own reasoning and conclusions, and if all else failed, I had three options left: Keep my mouth shut, lie, or run away.

So this doctor of psychology asked me some basic questions. I answered them, and then he tried to go deeper. I refused to talk for months, and then in my last session, knowing I would never see him again, I told him everything ever done to me. I thought, *I will never have to see him again, so he can never hurt me with this information.*

Soon, the original case worker who first took me from my mom's house showed up again. I had become too much for the foster parents. They were becoming physically abusive toward me due to my rebellion. I didn't know it, but my mother had exerted her parental rights and asked for me back after three years. I was terrified of going back home to her. I couldn't breathe. I thought

HE SETS THE PRISONER FREE ~ SHAWN HURLEY

that everyone would be happy I was leaving because of all my destructive behavior. I was surprised to learn that my foster parents never wanted me to go back home. I only found that out years later when I went to make amends with them.

But I saw myself as hopeless, unloved, and unlovable. I returned home to an unimaginable environment where my mother had grown even worse in the frustrations of her own life. She seemed to double up on her punishments, as if to make up for lost time. I became a sort of twisted therapy for her, where she could vent the anger meant for others on me, and she would find temporary peace.

I began to act on all the voices of my fears and all the twisted emotions that were overtaking me. My punishments became unbearable, which caused severe mental issues. In the summer before fourth grade, I escaped from my room four or five times. I was locked in my room for fifteen to twenty days at a time with no air conditioning and no fan with very little food and water. I stared at the walls day and night. I grew in anger and lacked any social skills due to the isolation. It all started to overwhelm me, and I became very introverted and very violent behind the scenes.

Everyone always loved my youngest brother. He was an adorable little boy and had a heartfelt story: surviving heart disease. He had a big scar on his chest from open-heart surgery that always garnered sympathy. It was no different when I came back home. I always felt like I had this invisible sign on me that said "Don't go near him. He's not worth your emotional investment."

A BAPTISM OF FIRE

My anger progressed internally. One day, I went to get my brother from the fire station next door. I walked in, and no one was around, so I went all the way to the back of the station, where I heard voices. The guys were watching TV and joking with my brother. I said hello and told my brother he had to come home. The firemen started yelling at me and told me to get out and not to come back. I hadn't done anything wrong. I was so hurt and so angry. What was wrong with me? I just wanted to be liked and accepted. I couldn't understand why people didn't like me.

My anger overtook me, and I lost all impulse control. As I was leaving the fire station, I saw a can of gasoline and proceeded to fill the boots that were lined up near the fire trucks with gasoline, hoping every one of them would catch on fire. My anger had been growing for years, but I was still very much afraid of being directly confrontational.

I continued in and out of foster care but now along with my brother due to mom's many surgeries from the ulcerations in her stomach and intestines. Mom's boyfriends came and went. Every one of them had their own sadistic style that I endured. My brother never had to endure the beatings, but it was no big deal anymore. I didn't feel anything emotionally.

That year, in fourth grade, I robbed my first gas station. I broke in through a window in the back and took all the change from the register. This was very impulsive behavior. I was just walking by, and the thought crossed my mind to rob it. Many of my fights and other destructive behaviors were also very impulsive.

HE SETS THE PRISONER FREE ~ SHAWN HURLEY

My moral compass seemed to shut down, and I was running on instinct and desire. Whatever idea I had seemed okay to do. Of course, I still managed to put on a decent front to the world, but below the surface, I was creating my own code of conduct. I was juggling fear and masking my self-hatred with many lies.

My Savior Appears

We moved to a new home, and my mom needed to hire someone to watch her kids so she could find another man to take care of her. So she hired an apparently prim and proper young lady to watch us. But she turned out to be dating one of the biggest drug dealers in our town. One day, they were passing this pipe around, and whatever was in it really stunk. I think this was in 1972. They thought it would be funny to let me smoke some too. For the first time ever, I was happy to be alive. I felt so, so free. I smoked that stuff and couldn't stop laughing and coughing. I had been trying to get the feeling it gave me for years: to remove the burden of all my troubled thinking. I finally felt like I fit in somewhere, and I couldn't wait to do it again. I wouldn't experience anything like that again for another year. The babysitter quit shortly after because my mother didn't come home for three days.

I fought more during this time and not because other kids were hurting or making fun of me. When I saw older kids intimidate and ridicule younger kids, causing them great fear, stripping them of any dignity or safety to express who they were, I fought these older kids and beat them down in order to humiliate them. I was just trying to protect the younger kids.

Unfortunately, on paper, I was labeled a troublemaker and unfit for any classroom or schoolyard setting. I had been expelled every school year more than once, and I had not even finished fifth grade yet. Guidance counselors tried to save me with genuine caring and all the tools at their disposal, as did well-meaning teachers.

I was on a path guided by emotional impulses and a warped moral code, a path that changed constantly to fit my own selfish desires. In other words, I wanted what I wanted when I wanted it. "No" was not in my vocabulary. I made up my own rules as I went along.

My Biological Father Returns

The return of my biological father would cause me some of the greatest pain I ever experienced, but unfortunately, that pain came in the form of pleasure that would continue into my adult life in the way I viewed woman, sex, and money.

He was an unassuming man, now age fifty-three and an all-around good guy who would help the less fortunate, especially single women with children who were struggling. He looked like a kind humanitarian, a humble bar-restaurant businessman who seemed to help those down on their luck. But the real man—the one that no one knew, not even his three previous children—was a sex addict, criminal, and murderer. Oh, some people knew that he

HE SETS THE PRISONER FREE ~ SHAWN HURLEY

ran some illegal games from time to time, but no one considered gambling to be a serious crime but just a good man's fault.

Maybe my father was looking to leave a legacy. Or maybe he was seeking to right some wrongs with his youngest child. But what he did was teach me how to destroy people and take from them through insincere kindness and manipulation. He taught me how to get people to depend on me so I could strip them of all their self-sufficiency and independence. He taught me how to control people through multiple avenues of basic human needs. The secret was to become everything they needed, whether it was lover, banker, or rescuer.

Slowly, over the next couple of years, I learned how to cook and run the restaurant. But along the way, my father taught me another lifestyle. Some teaching was on purpose; some was by watching him. Let's start with the women. This was my dad's usual routine concerning his love life, the one I observed very carefully. After picking me up on Saturday mornings, he brought me to the bar where I started working in the kitchen. The bar was always so exciting: the drunks, their stories of how great they used to be, and the drunk women, always willing to help a young boy out. Junkies showed up with their stolen goods, and the cops that my dad bribed always came for a free bottle of booze. My dad never wanted friends; it only appeared as if he did. He had a way of getting you to do whatever he wanted and making it seem as if it were your own idea.

A BAPTISM OF FIRE

We usually left the bar about 4:00 p.m. and proceeded to the house of girlfriend number one. Every week, she had a pound of cooked shrimp with cocktail sauce waiting for me. I watched TV while she and dad did their thing. Then on to girlfriends number two and three. Finally, we arrived at his place, and his neighbor had homemade food waiting for us. She also cleaned his place. This woman, he trusted.

At this time, I was introduced to pornography. Not only did my dad have every book in the world, he also made adult films. Dad was all about finding and knowing women who were struggling and needed money. He came to rescue them, but they always had to pay a price: sex. He was teaching me the value and power of money to those who needed it but didn't have it and the things they were willing to do to get it. By observing him, I was learning about women, sex, and how to get both through the use of money and manipulation. Even if these women had strong moral convictions, their need for money won out every time.

At about thirteen, these weird people called Christians moved into my neighborhood. I became best friends with one of their sons who was in the same grade as me, and he had the same attitudes as me toward authority. He made fun of it. Along with his older brother, we became partners in crime throughout our neighborhood. We were robbing local trucking companies and freight cars, along with stealing massive amounts of alcohol from the local distribution company. We had basically everything we needed.

HE SETS THE PRISONER FREE ~ SHAWN HURLEY

Their parents were Catholic charismatic Christians, and everything was about praising the Lord. I was always on my best behavior around them, but they weren't fooled. These two people would have an influence on God's plan for my life. I was intrigued because they were the only two people I had ever met whose actions lined up with their words. People often look for the hypocrisy in those who say they know Jesus, but I found none in these two, unlike all the others who said they knew Jesus.

When I turned fourteen, my dad thought it was time to have a new tutor of sorts as a rite of passage into manhood. One day, while working at the bar, a friend of dad's showed up. He was about twenty-five years younger than my dad and had just done ten years in prison for selling machine guns. He was the strongest, most violent man I had ever met, and everyone feared him except me and my dad. This man liked me right away and started to teach me everything I would ever need to know about people and how to hurt them.

He started with knife-throwing, a skill he excelled at, and I was an eager student. I practiced eight hours a day, and I soon became somewhat of an expert. While running full speed, I could pull a knife from my belt, fully twist in the air, throw it, and hit my target every time. I was very proud of my accomplishments. To be sure, we aren't talking about Little League baseball.

I'm telling you all these things and a few more so you can see my thoughts of who I really was and how I was wired through my life experiences. The boss of this world did everything he could to keep me from my destiny. You see, he knew that God chose me from the foundations of the world, and he was going to try to take my life before any of that had a chance to be a reality.

Finding True Love (Well, Maybe Not)

The summer just before I entered my freshman year of high school, I was in one of the most painful relationships of my life. It was just one of two where I ever felt pain, because I allowed myself to care. I should have never moved on from the eighth grade, but because I was so much trouble, I passed with all Ds. That was secret teacher code for "get out of our school." A very attractive eighteen-year-old senior was staying with friends across the street. I was sitting on my porch and saw her on crutches. So I walked over, and we chatted for a bit about how she injured herself. We quickly became friends, as I would occasionally help her while she was limited because of her injured leg.

One night, as we were talking, she leaned in and kissed me, just like in the movies. I instantly fell in love with her. We made love frequently, and she had my heart. But she wouldn't come around for weeks at a time. I was useless to the rest of the world while I sat on my porch hoping she would show up. My friends thought I was an idiot, but I just had to be with her. When she did show up, we would make love, and all my pain would leave. You see, I thought if someone was having sex with me, then that meant they loved me. All I wanted was to be loved, to be special to someone. Unfortunately, this woman was a female version of me.

HE SETS THE PRISONER FREE ~ SHAWN HURLEY

I later learned that this woman lived with another man. She had this broken part of her that liked to teach younger guys sexual activity; unfortunately, I gave her my heart, which she ripped out. I had gotten her pregnant, and she just moved away. I didn't see her again for two years. This strengthened my resolve to not trust anybody, especially women. At the time, my dad looked like a genius to me with his insight on how to take what you wanted with no emotional investment.

I began to regularly smoke weed and drink. I preferred the weed. It allowed me to function and made me feel whole. I dropped out of school after failing ninth grade but tried to go back the following year, only because selling weed was very lucrative at high school. I began to hang out with an older crew, stealing and dealing, robbing trucks and supplying my dad's bar with cases of liquor. The trucking companies and freight yard produced a lot of income.

I now spent more time with my dad catering big stag parties, and now that I was fifteen, the girls from the stag parties always provided some favors when the party was over, probably because of who my dad was.

The tension in my house became unbearable with my mother. She was always trying to exert her authority, but due to my need for independence and her personal insanity, I finally left home. My own addictions definitely contributed to the decision. I lived from place to place, crashing in basements and on people's couches. Dad's house wasn't an option. He was always willing to

A BAPTISM OF FIRE

spend some time with his children but resented anyone living with him.

I hooked up with a couple of close friends, and we went on a rampage of stealing and drug dealing. We began breaking into houses and fencing stolen goods. I soon landed behind bars. Unknown to us, the fence was working with police because of a pedophile charge hanging over his head. One day, as I was walking through a parking lot to meet two friends, detectives swarmed in from all sides, guns drawn like some crazy movie. Fortunately, I had just sold the two guns I had for a pound of weed and an ounce of hash. But I was arrested carrying the drugs.

I had never been arrested before. At fifteen, I felt defeated, but at least, these guys were the police, and I had rights as a juvenile. I was feeling cocky. Well, don't believe everything you hear about your rights. You have none inside the police station. I was beaten pretty badly and handcuffed to a chair in a room full of detectives. They wanted to know where I got all the drugs. I never gave up that information, although I did pay a heavy price with my first official beating.

Unknown to me, my mother had filed a stubborn child petition, and because of the many house break-ins and the drugs, I was sent to juvenile lock up. Needless to say, my dad was very upset. He always had this rule: If you're going to commit a crime, do it alone so that no one will know but you. You see, the fence that we were fencing goods to never saw me because my older friend always dealt with him. But my friend was the one who gave

HE SETS THE PRISONER FREE ~ SHAWN HURLEY

me up. I learned a valuable lesson and actually needed to learn one more. Never commit a crime drunk. That one took a while.

While rotting in juvenile detention, thinking about my future, a well-meaning social worker who was out to save the world from the injustices done to the poor and the afflicted came to save me. I faced the judge with reduced charges, as the drugs were never mentioned. I was remanded to the Department of Youth Services, and this quiet social worker offered me a proposition. "I'd like to get you out of lockup and have you visit a foster family that wants to meet you."

I said, "Sure, whatever!" I had a really bad attitude.

As we pulled up to the building in the south end of Springfield, the bottom floor to the left of this apartment block was boarded up and spray-painted with graffiti. We went up to the old, gray, weathered back porch. It would have given way if you leaned too hard against it. The social worker knocked on the door, and we walked in. Two ladies were sitting at the kitchen table, and one of those dogs that looks like a hot dog was barking. I just wanted to kill it. One of the ladies said, "Why don't you go down the hall and say hello to one of the foster kids that live here?"

I went down the hall and knocked on the door. This kid was smoking a bowl of pot and asked, "Do you want some?"

I said, "No thanks, I don't get high."

He said, "It's okay. The foster mother doesn't care."

I said, "Wait a minute. I'll be right back." The excitement was building as I raced back to the kitchen. When we pulled up, I had

A BAPTISM OF FIRE

told the social worker I wasn't staying in this dump, but he had persuaded me to at least meet the people. Can you imagine how happy he was when I came into the kitchen and said, "These people are really nice, and I think I'm going to stay"? He was elated, and now, his job was done. He had saved one more child.

It was a dream come true for a kid who hated rules. My only responsibility was to be home every two weeks to sign the checks she got for us living in her house. I quickly began dealing drugs, stealing from local businesses, and becoming friends with the women in the neighborhood. I must have been born stupid because one day, at one of the house parties, a beautiful blonde German girl and I became friends. In about a week, we fell in love with each other. She snuck out of her house, and we made love to each other. We spent all of our time together, laughing and partying. I found I had a horrible emotion, one I didn't know how to control: jealousy. It ruined everything.

We were both drunks in the making, and our tempers flared. Due to those tempers, coupled with my insecurities, she hooked up with someone else, which destroyed me. We had survived a pregnancy and a termination demanded by her parents. She was only seventeen, and I even bought her a diamond, hoping we would be married. She sent the ring back to me when I was later in jail.

Between the ages of fifteen and eighteen, I had no supervision and learned to live the Italian way—the criminal aspect of that heritage. As one of the only Irish kids on the block, I

HE SETS THE PRISONER FREE ~ SHAWN HURLEY

received many beatings until they figured out I wasn't going anywhere and that I hated the rest of the people on the planet as much as they did. I cut off all my long hair, learned a little Italian, and began a whole new life of crime and brutality. These sociopaths became my greatest friends. My goal in life now was to always be high and hurt as many men as I could. I led a very secret life that even my closest friends knew nothing about.

I also learned there was a pecking order in this culture of maniacs and an honoring of the men who were associated with it. But as usual, I had to learn the hard way. One day, while feeling my invincibility at seventeen, I was in a local restaurant telling this guy to get out of my way or I was going to wreck him. An argument ensued, and he rushed out. The waiters and my Italian buddies said, "You'd better get out of here."

I said, "What do you mean?" I then started to get this feeling like I had made a big mistake.

Suddenly, this man returned with another guy who can only be described as a mountain with a face that someone broke their shovel on. I was beaten and thrown into a pole outside the restaurant. That night, while hanging on the corner, one of the older guys came up to me and said, "I have a message for you. You were pointed out. Don't mess with that guy anymore." He didn't have to tell me twice. I found out he was a member of a Mafia family.

In those three years, I robbed everything and everyone I could. I hurt many people. I slept with every woman who would let

A BAPTISM OF FIRE

me. I hung out with dancers and witnessed some of the most violent acts you could ever imagine. I was arrested frequently for committing crimes. I was only caught when I was under the influence of alcohol, but unfortunately, I never made that connection. Fortunately for me, juvenile facilities were overcrowded, and my father had a good lawyer.

HE SETS THE PRISONER FREE ~ SHAWN HURLEY

Chapter 2
FROM DARKNESS TO LIGHT

What most young men wait for had finally arrived: my eighteenth birthday. I could now legally pursue my dreams as an adult. Some young men go to college; some join the armed forces. I could now legally drink. That year, I got popped for three felonies: a break into a mob associate's home and two drugstore robberies. I finally figured out I would be dead soon. I had no skills to live, and I was messing with the wrong people. Thank God for a friend who was a made member of this crime family. I was friends with his son. He stepped in and spoke on my behalf. I believe I am alive today because of that intervention and the grace of God.

I committed one of the drugstore robberies with my best friend. His parents were the Christians. The new car he had just bought wouldn't start when we were trying to get away, and the cops swarmed us. Once we were released from jail, we decided to

HE SETS THE PRISONER FREE ~ SHAWN HURLEY

flee and not appear in court. I was going to get time because of my record and even had a possible death sentence hanging over my head. Years later, I would learn of an intervention on my behalf.

We decided to go where all our friends went when they had legal troubles: Florida. So we got drunk and gassed up the car, and off we roared with our brand-new plan to build our brand-new lives. Trying to get to Florida was an adventure in itself. We left drunk with a hundred dollars, so there wasn't much planning involved. To save on fuel costs, we tailgated semi-trucks and allowed them to pull our little MG convertible by way of suction. You had to be so close to the backs of these trucks for it to work. If they ever hit the brakes quickly, we would have died instantly. Finally, we figured out we could just gas up the vehicle and take off without paying. Well, as we were trying to take off at one station, the car kept stalling. The station attendant took off running out of the station. The car finally started, and we were off, never realizing that a candy-apple-red convertible MG sticks out like a neon sign in the deep South.

About fifteen minutes later, with their guns drawn, the South Carolina State Police arrested us. We were thrown into a cell with three of the biggest black men I've ever seen. I knew this could not be good. Where we came from, there were clearly marked-out territories for whites and blacks. Not like segregation, more like territory that you didn't cross into unless you were looking for a fight. But we were blessed because these were three of the nicest guys I had ever met.

FROM DARKNESS TO LIGHT

We were heavily fined for our transgression. The trial was held in the backwoods in a gas station filled with rifles. I had to call my dad and tell him what my plan was, and he wired money and said he understood. He had trouble accepting that I was so stupid, but he financed my whole Florida adventure until I found work. We had big dreams of becoming rich and eventually coming back home, successful and financially secure. Our plan had one problem: wherever we went, we brought ourselves. I couldn't hold a job, I loved to steal, and I loved to party and be a part of the action wherever I was.

The clubs were hopping. Daytona Beach was one of those places people went to pretend that they were someone else, and the women pretended they weren't married. The women were loose and made that apparent. Most of them only had two-week vacations. We were the out-of-town big shots, living by whatever stories we made up, always larger than life.

To help fulfill that role, I had hooked up with a cocaine dealer who wanted to move major weight. But he got busted before I even started with him. I had a very difficult time showing up to work somewhere for eight-to-ten hours a day, especially when I stayed out all night drinking. Our time there was short-lived, as we were creating havoc in someone else's territory and stealing from the wrong people. We had total disregard for anyone, partly because we believed our own larger-than-life stories. Later, we accidentally found out that money was paid to get us out of the

HE SETS THE PRISONER FREE ~ SHAWN HURLEY

way. So we headed back to Massachusetts where, at least, we knew all the players.

I Need Help

In Massachusetts, we lived in a rented garage and had a few bucks. I was alone in that garage one day in the quiet, where I had a moment of truth and honesty and felt like I should pray. I said, "If there is a God, I need help." This strange, tangible presence and peace came over me. At eighteen years old, my life wasn't going well. I had nothing, and I was facing prison or at least jail, depending on federal charges. It was a sobering moment. The thought of God and all those prayer meetings my friend's parents made me sit through came to mind. I thought of the songs and the character of the people, and something started to happen inside me. I wanted that life, but I quickly suppressed that desire and shook it off.

I thought I only had one problem in life, the same one that I always had: not enough cash. If I could only get more money, that would take care of everything. I used to fantasize about hitting the lottery or becoming a famous author, but these were only delusions, as I never played the lottery and dropped out of school in ninth grade.

I arrived back home after three months with only a green trash bag full of my clothes and personal belongings. I caught a bus back to my dad's bar, only to find out he was on a drunken bender and at his trailer. The bartender gave me a few drinks, and I dropped off my stuff at the trailer. Dad gave me a few bucks, and I was on my way to get some weed and a few more drinks. When dad started drinking, it lasted for months, and that's all he did. He went through a half gallon of whiskey a day. His sobriety lasted for years, but when he fell off the wagon, he was useless.

I hadn't spoken to my mom in a while, so I called her. She was married to a new guy, but she kept her old place where I could hang out. I eventually called the police department to check on the warrants that they had out on me. "This is Shawn Hurley. Are you guys looking for me?"

The officer came back on the phone a few minutes later and said, "Yes, we could use you." I said I would turn myself in the next morning. I was tired. I turned myself in, and the DA wanted me remanded, but the judge wouldn't hear of it. He thought I was a nice Irish boy for turning myself in. God knew what he was doing. I, on the other hand, had no idea what I was doing because for the next month, I couldn't get high or drunk enough. I was killing myself.

I showed up for court, and the judge postponed my case for another thirty days. Something inside me said, *If I don't go to jail today, I will be dead.* I raised my hand like I was in grade school. "Your honor, do you think I could go to jail today?"

The courtroom broke out in laughter, and the judge said, "I think we can help you with that." I kissed my mother goodbye as the tears welled up in her eyes. This woman whom I hated for so long was the only one who showed up at all my juvenile and adult cases; she was now watching her son being led away in handcuffs.

HE SETS THE PRISONER FREE ~ SHAWN HURLEY

So we made our way to the county jail in the prison court wagon, all ten of us shackled together to be processed.

I only received a two-year sentence for the drugstore crimes. No federal charges were brought against us because we never touched the drugs, so only state laws applied. That was the one and only time I was grateful for not touching drugs.

A New Home

There you have it: a glimpse into a man starting from his childhood until his incarceration. A man determined to do things his way, an island unto himself, if you will. I trusted no one and lived by every thought that would bring me importance, reputation, and pleasure. I used and abused everything and everybody to get what I wanted. I was extremely self-centered, a god unto myself.

Unlike the rest of humanity, my selfishness was much more apparent, infringing on society's right to the safe pursuit of their own selfish lives. All of my best thinking, planning, and manipulation ended me up in jail. Once processed, cavity searched, and deloused (oh yes, just like the movies!), I showered and was given clothes and bedding and put in cell number fifty-eight, the third tier. They locked the door to this filthy ten-by-nine cell with the walls of peeling green bricks. My bed was a torn-up plastic mattress and pillow, and the cell also boasted a disgusting toilet and sink. I had my very own condo that faced the water treatment facility. That stink filled the jail every day.

The saddest part in all this was, I couldn't figure out how I ended up there. I thought I was a good guy. I didn't spit on old people. Are you kidding me? Our self-deception will blind us all the way to the grave. That's the lie I told myself. I couldn't see any of my actions or the lives I had destroyed. I judged my life on a self-made standard—my moral code—because I didn't spit on old people. Everyone should judge me on that standard of living and let me out of there. It was delusion at its finest. But criminals are like that. They can never assume responsibility or see the reality of their lives. I judged my life on my intentions, never on the reality of my actions.

As I sat on my bed, I thought about the reality of my situation. I was caged like an animal in a brick-and-steel building with all the rest of the animals, and I could not leave until someone came with a key and let me out. My life had been like a movie, and I was the director, producer, and star, writing the scripts as I went. But I didn't envision this anywhere in the original script. There would be no prison breaks like the movies. Now I was forced to do what I had always done: adapt to live and survive.

Suddenly I was snapped out of my moment of self-pity and reflection as a friend from my past passed by my beautiful window made of green bars. I yelled, "Hey!"

He said, "Oh, man, what in the world are you doing here?"

He put the word out I was in there; others began to stop by. And by the end of the day, I was hooked up with weed, adult magazines, and extra food from the kitchen.

HE SETS THE PRISONER FREE ~ SHAWN HURLEY

In my twisted mind, I said, *This isn't so bad. I can do a couple of years.* I was in such denial and void of any sense of responsibility for the reality of my life.

God had other plans for this wanna-be gangster—this idiot who had become a legend in his own mind. When you're in a jail cell, one thing you have is plenty of time to think. I started to think about life and some of the happiest times I ever had. One would think the happy times would have been the women or the money and drugs. But my thoughts always returned to that Christian couple and their family. They always had dinner together at night and did chores and went to church together and had donuts afterward, with everyone getting their favorites. They all had a place at the table and had order in their lives. They were fair and never lied. At prayer meetings, which I was made to attend, I even watched people care for others' needs.

Now as I sat with my thoughts, I wondered how people arrive at that point in their lives where they could be that kind and consistent. Surely, it couldn't really have anything to do with this person called God. Because the very religion they were practicing was the same one that others had practiced that beat and hurt me as a child. Somehow, they had found a part of that religion that looked really different. They called themselves Christians and worshipped Jesus. They loved each other and people like me who were unlovable.

I was very curious as my thoughts started to build a foundation of my happiest times. Was it truly possible that perhaps

FROM DARKNESS TO LIGHT

my life could be different? I decided to find out. It was obvious to me by my surroundings that I was not excelling at this thing called life. I wrote them a letter on some jailhouse toilet paper and asked about the Jesus that they knew. I gave it to someone to mail. Little did I realize that my life was about to change in ways I could never begin to imagine.

The Night of the Great Awakening!

That night on November 19, 1981, the guard stopped at my cell and gave me four pieces of mail. I hardly ever got mail. It was from the Christians I wrote to. The letter said, "If you want Jesus to come into your heart, ask him. He died for your sins on the cross, and he loves you." That's all I remember from the letter and that the paper was white and very thick with a beautiful blue backside. They also sent a book called *Prison to Praise* by Merlin Carothers, a born-again Baptist minister. I wasn't much of a reader, so I'm grateful that the book was thin and the title was catchy. The opening paragraph got me. The words said something like this: "I felt the cold slap of steel on my wrists." I could definitely relate.

My excitement was building as I read about the clever criminal life he was living and how he encountered God and the miracles that started happening. The strange thing was that I believed and hung on every word I was reading. I never questioned any of it.

I put the book down, and it was as if someone had removed a veil that was covering my mind. I started screaming, "He's alive! He's alive! It's all real! God is real! He's not just a church building.

HE SETS THE PRISONER FREE ~ SHAWN HURLEY

He is alive!" A million volts of electric love were streaming through my body. The presence and power that filled that cell and me could only be described as liquid, volcanic love.

The love I had searched for my entire life was flowing through me. I was being washed and loved. All my fear, guilt, shame, and condemnation were gone. God was with me. He was really with me. I tried to stand, but my legs couldn't hold me. I fell against the wall. I was burning up like a white-hot poker and started speaking in an unknown language. My mouth and tongue were moving so fast, I thought my lips would run away. I felt brand-new. All of my faculties were restored but better. I was filled with joy and hope, and although I was locked up, I had never been so free. It didn't matter where my body was—I was with God.

Some of the other prisoners were yelling, "Shut up, or we will kill you." But I couldn't stop worshipping him. I knew—I really, really knew—no one could hurt me unless God allowed it because he was with me. I was safe, and I knew it.

In between the yelling, my first prayer just flowed, telling God how amazing he was and how much I loved him. "I need a Bible. Send me a Bible." I kept saying this as I drifted off to sleep that night, a brand-new creation in Christ. Of course, I had no idea what happened, but I was not the same man. God was real and was with me.

The next morning, I woke up with God. I praised him and thanked him that he loved me and I loved him. I was so filled with love for everyone and so free of all the voices and the anger. My

FROM DARKNESS TO LIGHT

old life was gone. That old man was nowhere to be seen. I walked with God in the cool of the day, and I knew it.

A friend soon showed up at my cell with my first test. Of course, I didn't know it was a test at the time. He came to tell me his girl came through, and we were going to get good and high. We were waiting for her to visit so she could pass him some dope when she kissed him goodbye.

I said, "Reggie, I don't get high anymore."

"What? What do you mean?"

"I found Jesus! He's in love with me, and he loves you too." There was so much love in me and coming out of me that even my physical vision perceived life and people as brighter. I saw no categories but could only see through the eyes of love.

Reggie was stunned and could tell something had happened. I'm sure mental illness came to mind, but he just said, "Okay, cool. Take it easy, brother." Then he left.

"I don't get high anymore." My response was just automatic. Where did that desire go? Getting high wasn't in me or part of me. It wasn't part of this new man. It wasn't in his identity.

That night, as I was sitting in my cell, a familiar voice came down the tier. Before I knew it, a gentle man was outside my little barred window. He reached into his little wicker basket. "Would you like a New Testament Bible?"

I couldn't contain my enthusiasm. I screamed at him, "I just prayed for a Bible!" It was my first prayer, and two weeks later, God answered it. I didn't know that God hears all our prayers! The

HE SETS THE PRISONER FREE ~ SHAWN HURLEY

poor guy just slid the Bible through the bars and took off. I devoured the New Testament.

Every day, I was in prayer. I still had some daily flesh habits (playing cards and smoking cigarettes) as far as my jail routine went. But I didn't swear or fight, and I started telling anyone who would listen about the love of God. I started baptizing guys in their sinks. We asked Jesus to come into their lives after asking forgiveness for their sins. I was on fire! I had no idea what I was doing, but I was sure everyone needed God even if they didn't think so.

I had no concept of who Jesus really was or what had happened to me. I was just in love. As I read the Word of God, I saw that Jesus was healing people, so I tried something. My left index finger was crushed in a jeep accident after I had held onto the roll bar as the jeep flipped. I held my hand up to the ceiling and said, "God, will you heal my finger?" It started to bend. It was painful, but I bent it again and again, and it became easier. About two minutes later, I could bend it completely with no pain. It worked. Jesus healed me.

I spent long hours telling Jesus how wonderful he is and praising him. I spoke in tongues for hours. I was having supernatural experiences. For example, one afternoon, as I was praying while lying on my bed, I began to trail off to sleep. Suddenly, my body jerked up in the air like you see on TV when doctors try to shock the heart back to life. Something came out of me with three voices singing in a weird melody. To this day, I have no idea what that was, but obviously, something needed to leave.

Another time, I was at a Bible study with about fifteen other prisoners, and the Holy Spirit spoke to me. He said, "I want you to pray this out loud: 'Father, please show me in some audible or visual way that these prisoners believe in you.'"

I said, "No, Holy Spirit, that's not a good prayer."

I'm sure he laughed.

I argued with him, but when he told me a third time and used my name, I prayed for it. None of the men were too happy with me as I tried to tell the Holy Spirit that they wouldn't be.

Later that night, I was singing and praising God in my cell as I did every night. The acoustics in that old jail really made my singing and praising very beautiful. That night, I thought I was being really quiet, but one of the guards told me to shut up because people were trying to sleep. I said, "Yes, sir," and I stopped. He kept walking, and out of nowhere—with no open windows in front of my cell—a huge gust of wind blew right through me and filled me. I began singing at the top of my lungs. I had absolutely no control. I didn't know what was going on. Two guards came to my cell, shining their flashlights in my eyes. I was coming out of it and was not really sure of what was going on.

As they unlocked my cell, one of them said, "You're going to the hole."

Now I'd only seen the hole or solitary confinement in the movies. So I started protesting, "It's not my fault. It was the Holy

HE SETS THE PRISONER FREE ~ SHAWN HURLEY

Spirit. He filled me. I had no control." So now, I sounded crazy, but I was at peace inside even though I was sincerely presenting my case. I asked if I could put on some pants and grabbed my blanket.

As I was walking down the tier with my head hung low, I asked the Holy Spirit, "Why did you do this? I'm going to solitary confinement." I was very sad and confused.

Then suddenly in the quiet, from way down at the other end of the jail, someone yelled out, "Praise the Lord!"

Suddenly, three hundred prisoners were singing praises to God. My head quickly lifted, and the Holy Spirit reminded me of the prayer he had me pray. It wasn't to show me just the faith of the men in the Bible study but of all the prisoners. That's what he wanted to show me. Now I was joyfully walking to the hole with a certain type of Holy Ghost strut!

I was so filled with love and the overwhelming presence of God. They opened the door to the hole, which was a large dark cell, but when I stepped in, it lit up. Praise God! I turned to the men and told them I loved them both and forgave them. I did something that I would never do unless I were drunk: I danced and praised God like I was dancing in heavenly light and like a thousand angels were with me. It was an amazing night.

A guard came and woke me up, telling me to go back to my cell. What a relief—only one night in the hole. As I stepped through the solid iron door back into the main jail, an unassuming man was standing there. I had no idea who he was, but as the guard delivered me to his charge, he said, "Here he is, captain."

FROM DARKNESS TO LIGHT

This captain said, "It's a good thing for you that your father is paying me to look out for you. Last night's actions should have caused you to be charged with starting a riot. You should still be in the hole, and you would have been denied eligibility for prerelease. Now go back to your cell, and we'll pretend this never happened."

God Will Use Everyone Available, Won't He?

Every day, I was usually chasing down guys, telling them how much Jesus loved them. Some even accepted him, and then I would baptize them in their sinks. Guys who knew my former ways stopped at my cell and wanted to talk about God. I knew very little, but I knew that he loved them and had forgiven their sins. And for some guys, that was enough, coupled with the fact that they could see the change and joy in my life.

A couple of miracles happened. I received my GED scores, and they were the top in my class. God was working everything out. Shortly afterwards, I was approached about a pilot program. The jail started sending prisoners to college, and I was being considered for the first class in January. I wouldn't have been eligible for the program if I had been charged with rioting. I was accepted and was moved to prerelease. I had entered jail in October and was moved to prerelease in January with 75 percent of my freedom back.

During my first semester of college, I received a 3.8 GPA with a full class load. Apparently, I wasn't as stupid as I thought I was—maybe just too high in grade school.

HE SETS THE PRISONER FREE ~ SHAWN HURLEY

In June of that year, I was paroled. For parole, I needed a job, and with the resources at the jail, they found me one washing dishes. I was shortly on my way with my one green trash bag of worldly goods. I stayed with my best friend's family since they had been corresponding with me and visiting me in jail and teaching me about Jesus.

The Spirit of God and I were best friends. Life was filled with joy, and nothing seemed impossible. This was about to be the happiest year of my life. I even got a little apartment in a section of town that I grew up in for a hundred dollars a month. It wasn't anything great, but it was mine and was in a neighborhood where a lot of my old friends lived.

One day, while in prayer, the Holy Spirit said, "I want you to go to this certain local hospital and apply for a job." I was so excited because I didn't enjoy washing dishes. The next day I was off, so I went to the hospital and filled out an application and tried to piece together a decent work history. Then I saw it: the question. "Have you ever been convicted of a felony?" I answered as I was taught by the counselors at the jail. "I will explain upon interview."

The interview immediately followed, and the lady asked me, "I see you have checked the felony box. Can you explain?" I proceeded to answer and be honest with her and even told her I had been in jail and was currently on parole. She explained the hospital policy and how they did not hire convicted felons, especially those on parole.

FROM DARKNESS TO LIGHT

Now I was puzzled. She asked what was wrong. I said, "I don't understand because God sent me here to apply."

Her jaw dropped. "Oh, he did? Well, that's nice, Mr. Hurley! Have a good day."

I said, "You too, ma'am. It was a pleasure to meet you. Thank you." I was on my way.

All the way home, I reviewed the voice I heard speak to me that said to go. It was God, so I didn't understand what had happened. I acted in faith by going to the hospital and felt the rest was God's part.

As I was standing in my kitchen two days later, the phone rang. It was the woman from the hospital I had interviewed with. She asked if I was still interested in working there. I said, "Yes, ma'am! You bet I am!" Just like that, God opened a door that seemed closed and locked to me—a felon, but a son of God. I tell this story to guys locked up. If God wants you somewhere, every locked door will open.

I was all over the hospital. Happy and eager to help, I brought Jesus with me to every patient. I told people that Jesus loved them, and I always prayed when I sat down to eat my meals in the hospital cafeteria. People asked questions. I told them about what God had done for me.

I was also on the Catholic charismatic speaking circuit at huge churches, Sunday schools, and catechisms. Some priests wanted to write my life story, but other priests weren't so pure. I was approaching superstar status, a legend in my own mind. Many

HE SETS THE PRISONER FREE ~ SHAWN HURLEY

were being touched, and lives were changed. Your adversary, the devil, is patient, and sometimes, he will just allow others to do for him the work he wants to do in your life. So many people told me that I was amazing. Pride was quickly taking over, and I believed I was a cut above the rest.

I was now attending Catholic church and was on the fast track for the Franciscan Seminary as I thought and believed that the Catholic church was the true church of God and the ultimate authority. I immersed myself in their theology but quickly found myself filled with guilt, shame, and condemnation when I sinned, which propelled me to try to work my way back to God. I didn't know that God's people were the church. People were enthusiastically seeking me out because of my dramatic conversion, so I must be okay, right? Ugh!

I have a lot of amazing Catholic, Spirit-filled friends who I'm sure have never encountered this deception, but the devil had me hook, line, and sinker. This deception lasted for thirty years. It started with a small moral failure. But instead of asking forgiveness and believing I was once again right in the sight of God—based on his righteousness, not mine—I waited to *feel* right. I was instead calling God a liar and saying that Jesus wasn't enough. So now I was trying to work my way back to God when the truth was that he and I were one all along.

My freedom was gone as I based our relationship on my good behavior. I believed he only loved me if I was living right and morally. If I was living morally wrong, I knew he was mad at me.

FROM DARKNESS TO LIGHT

The enemy influenced my thinking. I then decided (with my will) to practice every vice that I had been freed from two years prior. As soon as I put that first sip of alcohol to my lips, my entire immoral thug life came flooding back, and my relationship with God turned into one of mostly hiding and begging for forgiveness.

I never knew about mind renewal and simply allowed the priests to dictate what a relationship with God was really like. I thought I would always be a sinner and thanked God for the sacrament of confession. The devil used that as my "get out of jail free" card for my flesh. I could do whatever the flesh desired, then go to confession, and I was good with God. I lived in this type of lifestyle for decades. I was filled with the Holy Spirit but living like a man who never knew God.

Very quickly, as the alcohol and drugs came back into the picture, I lost my job at the hospital. I wasn't allowed to enter the Franciscan religious order and lost two more jobs. I was now back into the life of getting high and dealing, sleeping with prostitutes, and raising Cain. I had become a full-blown liar and a thief again. I never stopped praying, but none of it was in faith; it was a strictly desperate act most of the time.

One day, by the mercy of God, as I lost my little apartment, someone told me, "It sounds like you're an alcoholic." It was actually a life raft for my drowning life.

I hid from Christians and only went to confession. Church was out completely; people were too happy, and I felt as if they could see right through me. Off I roared to detox, and once the

HE SETS THE PRISONER FREE ~ SHAWN HURLEY

alcohol and drugs were out of my system, I felt great. I was almost twenty-one, and the detox people suggested that I go to a treatment center. Considering I was homeless, it sounded like a great idea. I stayed clean and sober for about five months, and then in a freak medical incident, my lung collapsed, and I was given pain pills.

Soon I started to use again, and they kicked me out of the treatment center. My Christian friends, my best friends' parents, took me in, but I just kept getting high. I was such a mess. Then, one night, the grace of God intervened in my life. I was sneaking out the front door of their house to go drink with an old girlfriend, and as the door closed behind me, a voice spoke. "Do normal drinkers have to sneak out the front door to drink?" Truth and honesty collided, and I knew that I was an alcoholic. I didn't make the connection because God had supernaturally removed that devil from my cell. But now, I would have to follow the suggestions that I half-heartedly listened to in treatment.

The next day, I sat down with this couple and said, "I have to go back to treatment to get help with this." They had already known about my struggles for a long time and just kept praying. This time, I threw myself into recovery, and it worked. But I had so much to learn. I was trying to live by the spiritual principles that were laid out in this program, but it was hard. Even though I put down the alcohol and drugs, I had other addictions: women, money, shopping, food, and being a big shot (pride).

FROM DARKNESS TO LIGHT

I returned to prayer on a daily basis and even started going back to church. I started to become useful and reliable and to enjoy life again. I was working at the local detox and, of course, fell into lust with the night nurse, who was ten years older than me. I promptly moved in with her, and we set up house. In my first sober relationship, I thought I found the mother I never had. It was doomed from the start.

About three years into my sobriety, I was managing a retail store and lost my job. This woman said, "Why don't you go to nursing school?" This witnessed to my spirit. You see, when I was released from jail at nineteen, I applied to a college program and never showed up to do the paperwork because of the felonies. I had also begun to get high, so I had a lot of fear. Now God was about to bring me full circle, but I knew I would never get in. State law prohibited felons from becoming nurses because of the easy access to narcotics.

I tried to explain this to God in prayer, but he never answered me. I went and took the test to enter, and on the application, it asked if you had ever been convicted of a felony. Of course, I lied and said no. Imagine my surprise when, about a month later, the director of the program called and said, "Congratulations. You have been accepted to the class of 1988 nursing program."

I was thrilled. But I had to ask about the part on the application regarding felonies and criminal background checks. She said, "We have to do background checks on everyone to see if they

HE SETS THE PRISONER FREE ~ SHAWN HURLEY

have a criminal history before we can let them in. But as you already know, you have a clean record."

I said, "Oh yes, that's for sure." I technically didn't lie because God had wiped my record out of every computer bank. I *did* have a clean record.

My relationship was falling apart, and my girlfriend had already declared before I even started school that I would meet another woman there. She was right. I met my future wife, a woman waiting to be rescued. She was single with three children and an ex-husband who was a dope addict. She was tired of being alone. So I rode in on a white stallion, a knight in shining armor with my caring attitude and all the right words.

We were married a year after graduation with my first child on the way. We were perfect for each other. She was looking for someone to take over, and I was a control freak, so everything went smoothly for a while.

My first son arrived in 1989. Now I never thought that I was really capable of loving someone anymore, due to all the times I tried and was rejected or hurt. But standing in that hospital room, when my son arrived, I was overwhelmed with the most love I had ever experienced, other than being born again. Just the miracle of it. Four of us were in the room, then suddenly, there were five. That miracle just humbled me. I couldn't understand how a bum like me could have received such a gift.

A year and a half later, my second son was born—an equally beautiful gift. I would take him from the nursery every night and rock him and sing to him for hours. I was the most blessed man I knew. At this time, I was only going to the sober program infrequently, as life had gotten pretty busy with five kids at home. The financial strain was very difficult, and one day, an idea came to me about how to make money. Now that I was clean and sober, I could grow marijuana and sell it. I tried that, but it stunk up the basement. I hooked up with a much younger, well-connected man who could give me large quantities on demand.

We had recently moved out to the country, so I could drive into the city to do business, and no one was the wiser. Now, life got easier—at least financially—as I was making thousands of dollars on the side. We bought a house just up from the lake and also decided to continue taking in foster kids. We had been doing this for about a year at our previous location. I wanted to help kids in the same system that failed me. My head was in the right place, but unfortunately, my heart wasn't.

This sober life that I was living was contingent on the maintenance of my spiritual life, which was in the toilet. Now that I had become a nurse, I was in a field of lonely, broken caretaking women. I traveled to many different places through various nursing agencies. I had affairs with multiple women in these medical facilities almost every day wherever I went. I was such a mess inside. I wanted to be loved. I was addicted to wanting to be loved. This landed me in another program later on.

Eventually, all the hiding and lying caught up with me. One day, I said to myself, *I will have just one drink. What could go wrong?* I

HE SETS THE PRISONER FREE ~ SHAWN HURLEY

had plenty of money. I had made money in the stock market and thought I'd be just fine.

I became addicted to snorting cocaine and heroin, and a year later, I was smoking crack. In less than two years, my wife kicked me out. I ended up on the streets with two green trash bags and not a penny to my name. I became sick and was placed on Social Security disability because my esophagus was eroded away. I couldn't work anymore. I then met a woman with an apartment who fell in love with me. She and my mother actually took care of me through the surgery to my esophagus. They saved my life, but I couldn't stop using drugs for another two years. This woman also left me. She was tired of all the lies. Here I was, face-to-face again with the truth of my life.

She woke up one morning, and I had built an explosive device with no recollection of my actions. It was sitting on the coffee table. It truly was the end. I was alone, and by the grace of God, I was living in the house my wife and I used to own. Thank goodness for my mom, who paid off the foreclosure notice. My wife had moved out and took the kids to another town.

As I sat alone in the dark, I began to look at my life. I was in such a dark place, I figured I could never get my life back. I was too far gone for even God to save me. I thought about taking my life, but instead, I prayed from the depths of despair. I screamed, "*Help me! I can't do this anymore!*" The next day, I woke up and never had another desire to drink or take another drug. God had removed the spirit completely. I ran back to the twelve-step program. As of the writing of this book, I have had almost sixteen years of continuous sobriety.

As usual, I didn't know how to deal with my addiction to women, and I picked right back up where I had left off. I was quickly in another relationship with a woman who would get high on and off. God even healed me of my two serious illnesses—both physical and my substance abuse—and I was so grateful. But I couldn't stop all the sexual addiction.

I met a woman who was just getting sober at the same time as me. My ex-wife retained a lawyer, so now I had to sell my house because the kids wanted to live with me in the town they grew up in. I moved in with this new woman, and we set up a house. Our first date was going grocery shopping. She cooked for me every night and really treated me like a king. Of course, I was still a control freak, and we fought like cats and dogs. But she knew my love language; she cooked and cleaned and took care of me. Eventually, she, my youngest son, her daughter, and I left our small apartment. Nothing had really changed, although I wasn't drinking or drugging. But I had so many childish emotions and anger issues that living with me was like living with a case of nitroglycerin. One wrong move and everything would blow up.

She and I both were so immature, and due to her psychological issues, she was hospitalized many times. And when these chemicals in her brain were disrupted, she went back to getting high and not coming home for days. I finally had to leave. I couldn't take wondering if she was dead somewhere. People would

HE SETS THE PRISONER FREE ~ SHAWN HURLEY

steal her car, drain her bank account, and take her phone. I was watching her die. Every time she came back home, she was so thin and just a little closer to the grave. I really did love her in my limited capacity or, at least, cared deeply for her and her daughter. I finally had to leave her, but I would never just leave a woman unless I had another one waiting. I hated to be alone. You see, I was always looking for a mother to take care of me at home. Then I would be intimate with other partners. Of course, I didn't understand this at the time. When I looked back on my life, I saw the real man apart from all of my excuses and the blame I put on others for my behaviors.

Now most women, or even people who had a normal definition of love, would say I never loved this woman. Of course, they were right. This wasn't even close to love. But at the time, I had a very limited grasp of that meaning. My definition of giving love was if I took care of you and bought you things, it meant I loved you. Even though I was with other women, well, that was just sex and didn't matter. I was so delusional.

During these times, I often went to Mass and confession, still very wrapped up in Catholic doctrine and theology. My annulment from the church had come in, and I actually went to the Diocesan office and applied to become a parish priest. Even though I had children, I could still become a priest because of the annulment.

I figured that was my answer to all my problems. I could just put on priestly garments, and I would be holy and good. Now you can see that I knew absolutely nothing about God. I have read hundreds of books on the early church fathers, the saints, and the monastics. I owned thousands of dollars' worth of books, and I never got any closer to God.

Starting My Journey Home: God Sends Me a Woman

I moved out of a relationship of worry and pain and into one that would stretch me to the limits of my sanity, living with my new girlfriend, who would become my wife. When we met, I was already planning my escape from my last relationship. I had been sober for six years and had helped numerous people achieve sobriety by leading them through a program of recovery. I was also a very popular speaker, and young men actually wanted to be like me. I had a prominent position in the medical field.

When I met Kristina, I was sitting next to her and overheard a conversation that she needed money, which was usually the way I started romantic relationships. She seemed like the quiet type, looking for someone to lead her or be in control. Due to my own control issues, she seemed like the perfect match.

At first, everything went well. But as I tried to control everything, including her, I found out very quickly that she was far more independent than I first thought. Both of us had been through so much trauma in our lives that we were oil and water together. Our relationship quickly spiraled into arguments and fights.

Years later, a therapist told me that I treated my wife like a prostitute. We won't go into all the gory details of two very broken

HE SETS THE PRISONER FREE ~ SHAWN HURLEY

people coming together. Even on our wedding day, we were fighting over cake.

God sent this woman to destroy a wall that my ego and the applause of the world, both private and public, had built. This wall further protected me from all my fears and insecurities. You see, Kristina and I would plainly speak out about each other's failings, never acknowledging the good qualities that existed in each other. The fights that we had and the separations were all part of God's rescue plan for my life and hers.

When we married, I still had a horrible pornography addiction that lasted for years. I was even into sexting. She walked through all that with me. Six months after our marriage, she left because of all these issues, although we had almost broken up a couple of months earlier.

At this time, I wasn't following God, but I was heartbroken that she was gone and I was alone. As I laid on my bed in the fetal position, crying, I reviewed my past relationships, and the only common denominator in all the mess and pain was me. Maybe *I* was the problem. Just then, a voice of power and authority spoke to me out of the blue. "You will preach and heal all over the world."

I knew it was God, so I just said, "Okay," and went back to crying. I knew nothing about healing or preaching.

Kristina and I were separated through that whole summer. I finally started to adjust to her absence. I started to go back to the gym and work out and run. What I was really doing was getting

FROM DARKNESS TO LIGHT

into shape to find another woman because this one was gone and the pain of her leaving started to go away, just like all the rest of them. I figured she would never come back. She eventually filed a restraining order on me months earlier because of the angry messages I had left on her phone, and after she did that, all my feelings completely died for her. I struggled for years to forgive her for what she did.

HE SETS THE PRISONER FREE ~ SHAWN HURLEY

CHAPTER 3

SAVED AS A SON

One night, a mutual friend set up a meeting between Kristina and I, and we began to talk and reconcile. Eventually, we found a new place to live and got back together. However, my wife still had her own horrible issues that I wouldn't wish on my worst enemy. My wife's friend and spiritual mother had started going to a house church of Christians seasoned in missions and ministry, so we decided to attend. The small gathering was pleasant enough, but I wasn't motivated to return—that is, until I was about to leave. The leader of the group moved in extremely accurate words of knowledge. She pulled me aside to deliver a private and very personal word that no one else could possibly have known. As she spoke, I knew she was for real and that God was profoundly moving among these people.

HE SETS THE PRISONER FREE ~ SHAWN HURLEY

The more we went, the more I felt like I belonged there. I won't lie to you: Going to that house church was difficult because I had a lot of guilt and shame, and my wife and I were still consistently fighting, to the point where I sometimes hated her. But we persisted, and shortly after, the pastor announced they were planning a trip to South Africa. He said that if we were interested, we could go. I was so excited because I had always dreamed of traveling and had always wanted to go to Africa. What we didn't know is that as we tithed during the year, he put part of that aside to pay for mission trips.

As we arrived in Africa, I was filled with excitement and fear. My wife and I were fighting virtually the entire time. But God had put us together for a reason as our subsequent life together would prove beyond a doubt.

Three things about this trip were of life-changing significance. One afternoon, while standing outside a church before service, some women on our team had just returned from ministering at the brothels. They had arranged a Bible study for the prostitutes. They said the glory of God on those women was incredible. When I heard this, I was blown away: How could God move among people who, like me, were so steeped in sexual immorality?

I then heard the audible voice of God. He said the most important words that I would ever hear in my lifetime: "Do you see, Shawn? It's never been about you loving me. It's been about *my love for you.*"

SAVED AS A SON

Startled, I replied, "*You* love *me*?"

He said, "I never stopped."

That made absolutely no sense, because, according to the church and many pastors, I had disqualified myself from the kingdom of God because of the life I had lived. But now, *God himself* was telling me that *he* loved me. My life of darkness and dissipation was slowly evaporating in the whirlwind of his mighty love.

During our trip, we visited Michael's Children's Village, where, each day at noon, the destitute gathered to be fed. A group of amazing women would make a huge cauldron of beans and rice to feed the hungry. One afternoon, a man was in line. He was dressed in a suit; I am sure those were the only clothes he owned. My wife really wanted to give him her shoes, but her feet were too small. "Perhaps you could give him yours," she suggested. I wanted to oblige her, but two issues were stopping me. First, I had just bought these Nike sneakers for the trip, and second, I really liked them. Yes, I was selfish at the time. But also, my feet measure nine and a half inches, which is quite small for men. The man's feet must have measured twelve or thirteen inches, so there was no way my sneakers would fit him.

However, a great debate suddenly started in my head. A voice said, "Give him your shoes."

Another voice argued, "Oh, aren't you so holy! All your friends will think you're just trying to look special."

HE SETS THE PRISONER FREE ~ SHAWN HURLEY

Eventually, I couldn't take the internal conflict anymore, so I stood and walked over to the man. His feet were plainly too big, but that didn't prevent me from taking off my socks and shoes. In front of everyone and with great difficulty, I stretched my socks over his feet, and as I put his foot into the first sneaker, it miraculously began to grow. My mind could not comprehend what was happening because both sneakers fit him perfectly.

What is more, this man had never spoken, but now, he was sharing his life story with the leaders *in their language*. At one time, he had been a successful businessman but lost everything, including his family. However, in that moment, he was beaming with joy and love, and the happiness that those new sneakers gave him was amazing to behold. It was the first time I had ever encountered the three voices inside a man: the voice of God, the voice of reason, and the voice of the enemy. Two of those voices were designed to stop a move of God.

That South Africa trip changed my life in so many ways. A young lady demonically manifested, and, without hesitation, I tackled her in order to get my hands on her. She was like an animal, but people were casting out the devil, and because I felt I was made for this, I was compelled to join them. The devil was cast out, and she gained control of her right mind.

Returning home seemed too boring after what we had experienced, but I was now finally on my way back to a Father who loved and cared for me unconditionally. Something was being birthed inside me, so I volunteered to do a street-healing ministry with our little house church. I had no idea what it would entail, but as I was the only interested person, I quickly found out.

At the same time, my wife and I received a text from the lady who had initially invited us to the house church. **I have just come out of my prayer time, and the Holy Spirit said that your husband has the gift of healing.** As she knew my history, Kristina was totally unimpressed and skeptical. The lady pointed me to a book by a famous healing evangelist who worked in Africa in the early part of the twentieth century. The great John G. Lake also had healing rooms in the United States. I ordered the book, and I was so excited, I couldn't put it down.

Then, I got on the internet to look for more books, and I came across this young man with dreadlocks, healing people on the streets and filming it. His name was Todd White, and his spiritual father, Dan Mohler, was also online, preaching the most amazing message of righteousness and grace I had ever heard.

Pastor Mohler is a man so totally possessed of God's love that he has become a living incarnation of it. As I listened to him, my entire perspective began to shift in a way I never thought possible. He said that Jesus took my place on the cross *out of love for me*, that he became sin for my sake, thus canceling my penalty before God. He said that Christ and I were buried together and that I rose with him into a new life. I was now a completely new creation, born to a new and living kingdom. I was a co-heir with Christ of all the promises of our Father. All I had to do was believe it and live from that position. Through the blood of the cross, I

HE SETS THE PRISONER FREE ~ SHAWN HURLEY

was made clean in Christ. While I was *yet* a sinner, he came and died for me. But now, I was no longer a sinner but a *son of God*—a saint made in his own image and likeness. I had come to the point where I could see that old things had truly passed away. Behold, all things had been made new! Finally, I was no longer a slave to law but a child of grace.

Somehow, all this made sense to me because, in Africa, he said he had never stopped loving me. Therefore, I reasoned, he must see me apart from my sin actions. This opened within me a great hope. The more I listened to pastor Mohler, the more I knew I must follow and imitate his walk. His message was simple: make a prayer room, get alone with God, and start a relationship with him.

Although I didn't believe most of what I was saying, I started to repeat God's own Word back to him. I would declare that I am no longer a sinner but a son forgiven and right in his sight. I would exclaim how righteous I was because of Christ, and I would watch sermons and healings from many people who were filming miracles and putting faith into practice. Slowly, I was being transformed on the inside, as if I were being reconstructed internally to provide a dwelling place for God. Although he was within me since my conversion, I didn't believe that he was still there because I thought he came and went on the basis of my feelings. But now, as I started to believe God's amazing Word that we are temples of the living God, I began to feel his presence.

Moreover, I began to discern the voice of God above all the other voices chattering in my head. All these voices can sound the same, so it takes practice and patience to discern which is God's. In the early stages of this discernment process, failure is common. So, imagine my surprise when the Holy Spirit said, "You can heal people."

I replied, "Come on!"

He said, "No, you come on! I will take you on the streets and teach you."

All I could say was, "But God, I don't even *like* people!" In hindsight, this was my way of trying to get out of it because people scared me, and I was afraid.

But in his great love, he simply said, "I will teach you." God was speaking, because the devil never wanted to see anyone healed. Obedience was the only option.

So out on the streets I went, with no experience except watching some videos online. I decided to imitate Todd White. His approach was simply to say to people, "Your amazing God loves you and will heal you *right now*." Of course, I only said that when I felt courageous. Most of the time, I just walked by people because I felt foolish or because they looked mean. I dealt with great doubt, self-loathing, and personal moral failings. I allowed my emotions to dictate my self-worth, and so I reverted to making the flesh feel good. But as I continued to spend time in the prayer room before God, his love began to remove the fear of man. Consequently, each time I ventured out, I became bolder in approaching people as I grew in intimacy with the Holy Spirit.

HE SETS THE PRISONER FREE ~ SHAWN HURLEY

No one was getting healed, but I was now praying for everyone who would let me, and I was also going to places that would have formerly made me fearful. I was starting to believe, through my intimate time in the prayer room, that God wanted everyone healed. So I felt it was a matter of *when*, not *if*.

Finally, after offering to pray for people on the streets for two months, I placed my hand on a man with a back brace, and he was instantly healed. At first, I didn't believe him when he said he was healed. So I repeatedly prayed for him until he became annoyed.

That was in 2014, but now I faced a new dilemma: As I started to see people being healed, I returned home with these fantastic testimonies. However, because I had no evidence, my friends and family thought I was lying or, worse still, that I was mentally ill. My mother and brother went so far as to form a telephone committee because they believed I needed medical help.

All this, however, was about to change. One day, my wife and I received a phone call from a family member whose husband was in the hospital. After a routine examination, the doctors had discovered a large cancerous tumor in his colon. My wife responded to the news. "You know, if I tell Shawn, he will want to come and pray."

The lady said, "Actually, that's why I'm calling." At the time, the couple were not believers, but, when you have cancer, you will try even the crazy Jesus people! And so, I went immediately to the hospital where I worked to pray for her husband.

SAVED AS A SON

As I entered, I bumped into a friend who asked me what I was doing there.

"I'm here to heal my brother-in-law of cancer, in Jesus's name."

The look on his face said it all.

I entered the hospital room. The man looked as if he were dying, the cancer already doing its ugly work. He was ashen and very weak. Like a confident lead actor in a Broadway play, I took full control of the situation and commanded the devil of cancer out of him. In Jesus's name, I laid my hand on his abdomen. He said it felt as if something loosened. As my wife and I were talking with her sister, we happened to glance over at her husband, and it appeared as though someone had infused him with new life. His color had returned, and his countenance was glowing.

About a week later, my sister-in-law called us. The doctors had taken more scans to measure the tumor before starting chemotherapy, but they couldn't find the tumor! Neither were there were any cancer markers in the blood, so they discharged him with no diagnosis of cancer. As she told us this marvelous news over the phone, she complained of gout pain in her foot. There and then, I commanded her to be healed and told that spirit of infirmity to leave. Instantly, all her pain ceased. Shortly after, my wife's sister and her husband gave their lives to Jesus. What is more, my family no longer believed I was crazy.

Shortly after that amazing miracle, I put my phone number on social media. As I began to post about the miracles God was

HE SETS THE PRISONER FREE ~ SHAWN HURLEY

working through my hands, people began to call from all over the world. About 80 percent of them were being instantly healed of blind eyes, deaf ears, and broken bodies. But people also received emotional healing, and I was receiving words of knowledge—information from God—regarding intimate details of people's lives.

Soon, I was on the phone twelve to sixteen hours every day. I simply didn't know how to say no. As a result, my marriage suffered because there was no balance in my life and because I mistakenly believed that this work of healing was more important than anything else. Such mistakes are common when people start to move in divine power.

My wife is a very private person and enjoys the quiet retreat of home. I totally disregarded her wishes, believing that our house should be open to *anyone* who came for healing. Indeed, people came from all over the United States, and a couple even arrived from Canada. Yes, people were leaving with new livers; their cancers and diabetes were disappearing. It really was miraculous, but ministry should never have compromised the sanctity and security of our home. It took me many years to realize that this was wrong.

Another challenge in this new walk with Christ was a conflict with my nursing career. For almost thirty years, I was dispensing pills, learning medical procedures, and caring for the dying without much success. But now, it was totally different.

SAVED AS A SON

One afternoon, a woman called. She needed a new liver. The likelihood of her ever getting one was very slim, due to her history of drug and alcohol abuse. However, she received my number from a friend, and when she called, I invited her to come over with the promise that God would give her a new liver. She told me her story, and I explained how God loved her so much that he sent Jesus to die for all our sins. I placed my hand on her and commanded the disease to leave her liver. She became cold and then hot. Then, she left. About a month later, that lady went for a check-up, but the doctors were confused because her liver was perfect. But there is more to this astonishing story. I believe God healed her, not only because of his mercy but also because of what was about to happen.

One night, after an automobile accident, her thirty-year-old son was in a coma at the largest teaching hospital in our city. The physicians in charge of the brain injuries and comatose patients' ward spoke with her. "We are advising you to let us pull the life-support systems because we have never seen anyone wake up from a coma of this severity. And if, by some miracle, he does wake up, he will be a vegetable."

The lady called me when I was teaching an amazing man of God how to move in healing, so I brought him with me, and we laid hands on her son. We commanded his brain and body to be healed and commanded that he wake up. The family thanked us, and we left. About a week later, the boy woke up but with volatile behavior. So we returned to the hospital and laid hands on him

HE SETS THE PRISONER FREE ~ SHAWN HURLEY

again, this time, commanding his anger to go and his brain to be healed.

We heard no more until a couple of months later, when I received a call from this young man. He said, "My mom wanted me to call to say thank you for praying for me." It was the boy, and he was completely healed.

At that time, my pastor was planning a trip to Peru, and he asked me if I wanted to join him. Of course, my first mission to Africa was life-changing, but now, I was moving in power, so I couldn't wait to get there to heal every sick person I saw. I felt like a general in the army of Jesus Christ. We landed in Lima, and from there, we went to different villages and neighboring cities.

The miraculous was on the move. A child was brought to me who had never spoken a word. I cast out the spirit, and the little girl went and played with the rest of the children. That night, everyone I touched in that little house was healed. But as we were closing in prayer, they formed a circle and prayed for *us*. When I opened my eyes, the little girl I had earlier prayed for was standing in front of me. I took her in my arms as they prayed, and she began to speak! She shouted, "Mommy, Mommy!" and her mother began to cry uncontrollably.

And miracles continued for the rest of the trip: Deaf ears were opened, blind eyes were restored, and broken bones were healed. Devils were cast out, and on Sunday morning at our organized service, at least a hundred people were in my prayer line. They finally convinced me to stop praying after three hours.

SAVED AS A SON

One night in a mountainous village, I was preaching to some extremely poor people. As I listened to their pastor speak, a white sheet on the wall in front of me caught my attention. The Holy Spirit spoke to me. "That is how I see my people every day: clean and white like that sheet." What a beautiful revelation that was, especially as I had been struggling with thoughts of guilt and condemnation. He also said, "I am giving you everyone in this village. They will all be healed tonight!"

I then turned to my interpreter as I was suddenly filled with the power of the Spirit. I told her to hold out her hands, and, when I placed mine above hers, she exclaimed, "It feels like magnets pulling stuff out of me! I'm healed. I'm healed!" Up to that point, I hadn't known anything was wrong with her. After that, everyone in the prayer line was healed.

Back in the United States, I was at work, beginning my nursing shift. Trying to make ends meet had left me exhausted. I was sitting in my car in the parking lot, and I screamed out to God, "You have to help me financially! I can't keep working overtime and ministering full time. I'm so tired!"

About ten minutes later, I received a text message from a woman in Alaska. Six months earlier, I had prayed for her mother to be healed after a difficult knee surgery. After I prayed over the phone, the mother cast aside her wheelchair and walked down the hall. The text from her daughter said, "I was just in prayer and the Lord told me to support you financially." She sent me a check for $1,840.

HE SETS THE PRISONER FREE ~ SHAWN HURLEY

My joy was so great that I brought it to my prayer room. The Holy Spirit said, "I want you to get on the IRS website and start a nonprofit organization. Call it Happy Hands." When I asked why, he said, "Because when you put your hands on people, they are happy and you are happy." When I said that I didn't know anything about computers, he walked me through it all. Shortly after, I received an approval letter from the IRS, and Happy Hands Ministries was born. Not much money came in for a long time, but whenever the Holy Spirit wanted me to go on a missions trip, enough came in for my wife and me to travel.

Still, you can imagine some of the challenges that confronted me, especially in the medical field. To my supervisors and the doctors, I was something of a joke. But the Holy Spirit would invariably show up and disprove their assessment of me.

The following is a perfect example. My boss invited me to a social gathering of nursing managers. During the event, I was speaking with a woman who oversaw the Adult Day Care unit. I had prayed for her many times, and even some of her family members had been healed. She introduced me to the head of her clinical staff and said that I traveled all over the world. When they asked where I was going next, I said I was planning a trip to Africa. The lady in charge of the clinical staff asked me to explain what I did on such trips. I said, "I travel, feed the poor, and clothe them. I pray for the sick and God heals them."

Sarcastically, she countered, "Oh really?"

SAVED AS A SON

I asked if she needed healing for anything. "I will pray, and God will heal you right now."

Angrily, she responded, "I am fifty-three and in constant pain all day long. I need a hip replacement, and the pills that I take every day are destroying my liver. Sooner or later, I will need a liver transplant. Can God heal that?"

Quietly and matter-of-factly, I said, "Sure, he will heal you right now. Can I have your hand?" She looked at me with disgust but nonetheless gave me her hand. I commanded the pain to leave her hip, and then I asked her to check for pain. She began to move her body and scrunched her forehead. I smiled. "There's no pain."

"No," she said.

"God just healed you because he loves you. He is alive and continues to heal, just as he did two thousand years ago." I then received a word of knowledge about her back. "You have constant back pain, don't you?"

"Yes, I do," she replied.

"You have a short leg. Come with me." We walked into a hallway, and I asked her to sit against the wall. Her right leg was almost two inches shorter than her left. "I'm not going to touch you. I am just going to command it to grow, and God will do it. Just watch. In the name of Jesus, right leg come out *now*!" The leg shot out, and she gasped. She stood up, checked her back for pain, and then began to cry. That lady realized that there could only be one answer: God. For the first time in many years, she was pain-free and happy.

HE SETS THE PRISONER FREE ~ SHAWN HURLEY

When we returned to the party, the Holy Spirit prompted me to ask about her liver. We were back in public, so I told her I would be an undercover Christian and simply point at her liver and it would be healed. As I did so, she exclaimed, "What's happening? My whole body feels like it's on fire!" Her face had turned a deeper shade of red. A short time later, she went to her doctor, only to find that she had a brand-new hip and a perfect liver as shown in a scan. Today, that same lady runs five miles every day.

A Son of God

These are only a few stories of thousands that testify to the miraculous power of God moving through one ordinary man. He was a man who was lost—*so lost* that he would have gladly eaten swine food. He was down and out, left for dead, and consumed by drugs, despair, and the constant thought of perpetual damnation. He did not know how to love but merely how to use, steal, and destroy. But he was also a man who was loved from the very foundation of the world. Despite all the darkness that pervaded his life, that man was destined to reign as a son of his heavenly Father.

"It was never about your love for me, Shawn. It was always about my love for you."

Every day, he waited for me to come home. Amid all the horror, he never stopped loving me. He stood gazing out toward the horizon, knowing that one day, a lonesome figure would return to the place he belonged. I was the lost coin, the lost sheep, and I was worth leaving the other ninety-nine to pursue. (See Luke 15.) And pursue me he did until I was finally ready to come home. But even then, no reproach, no punishment, no guilt was laid upon me. I was totally forgiven, my sins washed away by the blood of the slain Lamb, Jesus. He killed the fatted calf, dressed me in the finest robe, and placed his ring upon my finger. For that is the nature of our Father: pure, excessive love.

Today, I walk in his power, not because I am special or privileged above you or anyone else. I do so simply because I *know* that I am his son and that he loves me. And how do I know that? Because he tells me throughout his Word. And if he tells *me* that, then he also says the same to *you*.

> For those who are led by the Spirit of God are the children of God. The Spirit you received does not make you slaves, so that you live in fear again; rather, the Spirit you received brought about your adoption to sonship. And by him we cry, "Abba, Father." The Spirit himself testifies with our spirit that we are God's children. Now if we are children, then we are heirs—heirs of God and co-heirs with Christ, if indeed we share in his sufferings in order that we may also share in his glory. (Romans 8:14–17)

Believing that astonishing fact is the key to unlocking the treasures of the kingdom in your life. I will devote the rest of this book to how to believe. It means becoming love, for that is the only way to bring light where it needs to shine.

HE SETS THE PRISONER FREE ~ SHAWN HURLEY

PART 2
OUR STORY

CHAPTER 4

A NEW CREATION

I was a prodigal who became a son. Or, rather, I was a prodigal who came to realize that he was *already* a son. And, if a son, then an heir of all that my Father possesses. Therefore, I came home, not to condemnation or punishment but to a father who lavished his unconditional love upon me. I didn't have to do anything to earn his love; it was mine *simply by virtue of being a son.* My life of immorality and depravity brought me to ruin. I, too, would have gladly eaten the pig swill. But even in those darkest moments, when the light of life had all but been extinguished, I heard these precious words deep in my soul: "Shawn, come home, for I have never stopped loving you."

As I pointed out earlier, this is the beautiful grace of God, his *free gift* to those who long for the peace that surpasses all understanding. It is a grace so deep and so great that the Father of mercy substituted his own Son for you on the cross of Calvary.

HE SETS THE PRISONER FREE ~ SHAWN HURLEY

What love is this that it gives up everything in pursuit of you and me, no matter how far we have strayed? It is the love of a father who predestined us from the foundations of the world, the love of one who will wait with everlasting expectation for his children to turn toward home.

You, too, can claim the glorious promises of the gospel by accepting that you are saved by grace through faith and that you are a coheir with Christ of the Father's kingdom. That is why the question of identity is so central to the Christian life. In the story of the prodigal, the father did not hold *any* of the son's transgressions against him. The wayward son identified himself as a sinner:

> "The son said to him, 'Father, I have sinned against heaven and against you. I am no longer worthy to be called your son.'
>
> "But the father said to his servants, 'Quick! Bring the best robe and put it on him. Put a ring on his finger and sandals on his feet. Bring the fattened calf and kill it. Let's have a feast and celebrate. For this son of mine was dead and is alive again; he was lost and is found.' So they began to celebrate. (Luke 15:21–24)

He did not denounce the prodigal as a disgusting sinner but joyfully welcomed his child as though he had never sinned. And that is how our heavenly Father sees you on account of the glorious sacrifice of his only begotten Son, Jesus Christ. The son

A NEW CREATION

was undeserving of his father's favor, and yet he received it freely and unconditionally. In the book of Romans, the apostle Paul explains that we are all in the condition of the prodigal son, saying, "But now apart from the law the righteousness of God has been made known . . . . This righteousness is given through faith in Jesus Christ to all who believe . . . for all have sinned and fall short of the glory of God, and all are justified freely by his grace through the redemption that came by Christ Jesus" (Romans 3:21–24).

Put simply, we are made righteous (justified), spotless, and wholly without sin, not because of anything we did but because of everything the Father did for us through Jesus. Our righteousness—or right standing before God—is a gift of love made manifest on the cross. We did not deserve it or do anything to merit it, and yet simply by faith, he eliminates our guilt and makes us right with him. Just as the prodigal son received his father's favor without earning it through works, so, too, we unconditionally receive our heavenly Father's grace and favor. It cannot be earned. It can only be bestowed upon us when we no longer rely on our own works but on the finished work of Christ. (See Romans 4:5.)

All of the guilt and power of sin has been cut away from us because of what Jesus did on our behalf (Colossians 2:11). Moreover, "He forgave us all our sins, having canceled the charge of our legal indebtedness, which stood against us and condemned us; he has taken it away, nailing it to the cross" (Colossians 2:13–14).

HE SETS THE PRISONER FREE ~ SHAWN HURLEY

Before accepting Christ as our Savior and Redeemer, we were sons of Adam—the first man. We were children of the fall, separated from the Father by sin. We were sinners without hope of salvation. But then, in his great mercy, Christ elected to reconcile us to the Father by paying our sin debt. Paul writes, "for the wages of sin is death" (Romans 6:23), indicating that we must pay for sin with our lives. That is the glorious gift that Jesus gives us: He pays *our* debt with *his* life. He takes our place so that we might come home to the Father. Through his blood, we are washed clean of sin and made perfectly righteous.

Paul explains, "But God demonstrates his own love for us in this: While we were still sinners, Christ died for us" (Romans 5:8). He substituted himself for us on the cross, crucifying and killing our sin nature that we inherited from Adam. "God made him who had no sin to be sin for us, so that in him we might become the righteousness of God" (2 Corinthians 5:21). Therefore, everything we once were in Adam has been nailed to the cross. "For we know that our old self was crucified with him so that the body ruled by sin might be done away with, that we should no longer be slaves to sin—because anyone who has died has been set free from sin" (Romans 6:6–7). Put simply, by taking into himself our old, Adamic, sinful nature and by nailing it to the tree, Christ set us free from sin and all its evil effects. Such is the radical beauty of grace—the free gift of a Father who loves us beyond measure.

Therefore, when Christ died, our sinful nature perished along with him. As the Bible states, "We were therefore buried with him

A NEW CREATION

through baptism into death in order that, just as Christ was raised from the dead through the glory of the Father, we too may live a new life" (Romans 6:4). As such, "if we have been united with him in a death like his, we will certainly also be united with him in a resurrection like his" (Romans 6:5). Paul insists at least three times in Romans 6 that we have been *set free from sin*. Hence, we must now consider ourselves "dead to the power of sin and alive to God through Christ Jesus" (Romans 6:11 NLT).

Through grace, we have been saved, because Christ freely did the work of salvation. He redeemed us from slavery to sin through the cross. All we must do is accept the gift of his love in order to be set free from the law of sin and death. Like the prodigal, all we must do is accept the robe and ring of righteousness and take our rightful place at our Father's table. This is what happened to us when grace was lifted up on the tree: "For what the law was powerless to do because it was weakened by the flesh, God did by sending his own Son in the likeness of sinful flesh to be a sin offering. And so he condemned sin in the flesh, in order that the righteous requirement of the law might be fully met in us, who do not live according to the flesh but according to the Spirit" (Romans 8:3–4).

We died with Christ, only to be raised with him as something completely new. Sin was canceled, and we were reconciled to the Father, no longer as sinners but as sons—those through whom the Anointed one now lives. As Paul proclaims, Christ "is your life" (Colossians 3:4). *Christ is now my life!* I am in him and he in me.

HE SETS THE PRISONER FREE ~ SHAWN HURLEY

"Therefore, if anyone is in Christ, the new creation has come: The old has gone, the new is here!" (2 Corinthians 5:17).

The cross killed who we were in Adam. Christ raised us up—not as forgiven sinners but as a *new species*. The new creation reality is the single most astonishing revelation of the New Testament, for it shows the power and love of the Father for his fallen children: "This son of mine was dead, but now he is alive!" The Father quite literally kills the old self and raises up a completely new self, devoid of any stain of sin. Our fallen DNA is rendered powerless, only to be replaced by the same spirit that raised Jesus from the dead. "But because of his great love for us, God, who is rich in mercy, made us alive with Christ even when we were dead in transgressions—it is by grace you have been saved. And God raised us up with Christ and seated us with him in the heavenly realms in Christ Jesus" (Ephesians 2:4–6). My Adamic DNA has been replaced by that of Christ Jesus. What amazing grace!

Through Adam, I died to God; but through Jesus, I was resurrected back into the family of my Father. We were sons of Adam, living in sin, but now Christ has reconciled us to God in one body through the cross, "no longer foreigners and strangers, but fellow citizens with God's people and also members of his household" (Ephesians 2:19).

Now, we have complete union with our Father because his life is our life. Paul tells us that "whoever is united with the Lord is one with him in spirit" (1 Corinthians 6:17). Therefore, "if Christ is

A NEW CREATION

in you, then even though your body is subject to death because of sin, the Spirit gives life because of righteousness" (Romans 8:10).

"Now if we are children, then we are heirs—heirs of God and co-heirs with Christ, if indeed we share in his sufferings in order that we may also share in his glory" (Romans 8:17). Christ is the "firstborn among many brothers," and we were predestined by our Father "to be conformed to the image of his son" (Romans 8:29). As such, we are filled with God as Christ's fullness flows from within us. Christ is the hope of our glory, and we are saturated with his Spirit. Paul pushes this to its marvelous conclusion when he declares that because his fullness overflows within us, "we have the mind of Christ" (1 Corinthians 2:16). Through spiritual discernment, his thoughts can become our thoughts. If his Spirit flows through us, we can live, think, and act as he did. And that is because, in the astonishing words of John the apostle, "as [Jesus presently] is, so are we in this world" (1 John 4:17 NKJV).

This is why understanding who you are in Christ is the key to walking in the Spirit. If you still think that you are a sinner and not a son, you will inevitably live your Christian life in guilt, shame, and condemnation. If you still believe that you must earn God's love rather than accepting it as a free gift, you will continue seeing yourself as separate from God and under the law of sin and death. So we must keep our eyes fixed on the cross, always as our starting point of relationship.

HE SETS THE PRISONER FREE ~ SHAWN HURLEY

Naturally, being set free from sin by his precious blood does not mean that we can now freely sin or do whatever we want. As Paul rhetorically inquires, "We are those who have died to sin; how can we live in it any longer?" (Romans 6:2). We ought instead to present ourselves to God in love and service to him as new creations, predestined to do the will of the Father. No wonder Paul exclaimed with sheer joy: "If we are 'out of our mind,' as some say, it is for God!" (2 Corinthians 5:13).

CHAPTER 5

LOVE NEVER FAILS

Healing, prophecy, and power began to flow in my life when I resolved to become like him. Of course, this does not mean that you try to become God, but you simply acknowledge that as his child, you will naturally share his characteristics. The most vital characteristic and the source of all power in a believer is *love*. John writes that "everyone who loves has been born of God and knows God … because God is love" (1 John 4:7–8). Later in the same chapter, he says that "if we love one another, God lives in us and his love is made complete in us" (v. 12). If, therefore, God's nature is love, then it follows that love will also define his children.

The whole goal of our instruction is love, according to Peter. John declares that "no one who is born of God will continue to sin, because God's seed remains in them; they cannot go on sinning, because they have been born of God" (1 John 3:9). Put

HE SETS THE PRISONER FREE ~ SHAWN HURLEY

simply, you cannot be of God and not love, for that is to deny your own nature.

As you have read, my whole life was one of selfishness and abuse of others. Even after the Holy Spirit swept through my prison cell, I continued to live a self-centered existence and cared little for the needs of those I encountered. Only when I seriously accepted Jesus's invitation to follow him did my life radically change. But that only happened when I realized that following him is not like following a baseball team. It means becoming who he is and doing what he does. It means being love for everyone you meet, whether good or bad. It means giving what you do not have, praying when you least want to, and going places when you would rather stay home. It means taking up your cross and surrendering your life totally to him—that beautiful example of perfect love.

"My command is this: Love each other as I have loved you" (John 15:12). This is why Paul tells us that we must be rooted and grounded in love and why he instructs that, above all else, we are to put on love, which is the bond of perfection. To abide in love is to abide in God because God is love. In other words, *You will never walk as he walked unless you become one with him through love.* If you want power, become love. If you want signs and wonders, become love. If you want prophecy and tongues, become love. If you want to heal the sick, raise the dead, cast out demons, and cleanse the lepers, then, yes, you guessed it, *become love*!

This has been the greatest revelation of my life, and I return to it every day. You see, becoming love is not something that happens once and for all. Indeed, in some cases, blessed people experience a second work of the Spirit and use many terms to describe this, including a baptism of love. For most of us, however, love is the *goal* of our instruction rather than something we readily possess.

However, we must still contend with the flesh. This explains why Paul exhorts us to "not lie to each other, since you have taken off your old self with its practices and have put on the new self, which is being renewed in knowledge in the image of its Creator" (Colossians 3:9–10). Hence, each day, we must put off the old self by practicing love. We do this, not through willful self-control, but by realizing that if he has forgiven us of everything, it is but a small matter to forgive others their sins against us. Put another way, *love always puts the other first* because you don't *need* to be first.

Why is that? Because in giving up his only Son to set you free, God proved his unconditional love for you. You have everything you could ever desire in his love. He is the source of your identity and security, which means that you don't need the affirmation or the applause of the world. When you know who you are in him, you then lay down your life to serve others. You let their needs become yours because your needs are already met in him. His love for you is the basis of your love for everyone else.

If you doubt the importance of love as the foundation of the new-creation reality, look to the words of John. "We know that we have passed from death to life, because we love each other. Anyone who does not love remains in death" (1 John 3:14). In

HE SETS THE PRISONER FREE ~ SHAWN HURLEY

other words, the proof that we have been saved is that we love. The proof that we died to sin with him on the cross and rose to new life with him in his resurrection is that we love. Or as Paul puts it, "hope does not put us to shame, because God's love has been poured out into our hearts through the Holy Spirit, who has been given to us" (Romans 5:5). In other words, love is the expression of God's nature as it manifests in his children.

When I step out to heal or encourage people, I seek to look at them through the eyes of love. This means that I look beyond any external imperfections and see only the perfection of Christ shining in them. Such is the nature of compassion, which is love in action. You strive to see beyond the anger, frustration, or the darkness that sometimes surrounds a person. You look behind the mask and see them in all their vulnerability. That is the love of God, for it doesn't consider outward appearance. You simply see them as Jesus would, and you love them accordingly. Isn't that difficult to do? Of course, but the key is to remember what Paul declares in 1 Corinthians 13: "Love never fails." When you live and act in love, when you realize who you are in Christ and let that flow, *you cannot fail*, even if you are rejected or abused. Something good will inevitably come from any act of godly love, even if you never get to see it.

Beyond miracles, beyond prophecy, beyond healing, beyond teaching, and beyond speaking in tongues is love. Paul says it is "the more excellent way."

LOVE NEVER FAILS

> If I speak in the tongues of men or of angels, but do not have love, I am only a resounding gong or a clanging cymbal. If I have the gift of prophecy and can fathom all mysteries and all knowledge, and if I have a faith that can move mountains, but do not have love, I am nothing. (1 Corinthians 13:1–2)

This is quite astonishing because Christ himself said that "if you have faith as small as a mustard seed, you can say to this mountain, 'Move from here to there,' and it will move. Nothing will be impossible for you" (Matthew 17:20). But now Paul is saying that if you have Christ-like faith devoid of love, you are nothing. Without love, all the following are ultimately useless: miracles, tongues, martyrdom, sacrifice, and faith. You gain nothing because, in the end, neither faith nor miracles will work apart from love. As Paul puts it elsewhere, "For in Christ Jesus neither circumcision nor uncircumcision has any value. The only thing that counts is faith expressing itself through love" (Galatians 5:6).

How does faith work through love? It works because when your motivation is love, what you have faith for is much more likely to manifest. That is why the Scripture boldly states that faith, sacrifice, martyrdom, and prophecy are all for nothing without love. Faith flows, on the other hand, when we are patient, kind, and humble. It flows when we don't insist on getting our own way, when we avoid anger, irritability, and resentment. It flows when we

HE SETS THE PRISONER FREE ~ SHAWN HURLEY

have compassion—*deep* compassion—for those in need. Love will offer that help without thought of reward, without thought of self-gain, or even without thought of manifesting a miracle. Of course, miracles will naturally happen through love, but that should never be the motivation *for* love. Love, you see, is its own reward.

I will say more about healing later, but for now, understand that, above all else, love heals. Why? Because the Christ who is in you, your hope of glory, is perfect love. As such, to heal in the name of Jesus is to heal in the name of love, and the power that imparts the healing is the love that has been shed abroad in our hearts by the Holy Spirit.

Put simply, the Christian walk is one of practicing love. In any given situation, the question "What would Jesus do?" could also be stated "What would love do?" Love will always put the other first, love will always lay down its life, love will never seek its own, and love will never take account of a suffered wrong. Love is my new nature. We have been spiritually recreated as love, which is the primary characteristic of our new identity. This means waking up each morning, focused on putting off the old and putting on the new. It means waking up to become love. That is what it means to grow in Christ. But if you are to grow in Christ and to realize your new identity as a son of love, you must spend time learning from love. Such is the beauty of intimacy, for without it, we can never claim to truly know God's voice.

CHAPTER 6

THE VINE AND THE BRANCHES

The Scriptures tell us, "Blessed be the God and Father of our Lord Jesus Christ, who has blessed us with every spiritual blessing in the heavenly places in Christ, just as He chose us in Him before the foundation of the world, that we should be holy and without blame before Him in love" (Ephesians 1:3–4 NKJV). *He chose us in Christ before the very foundation of the world.* He always intended for the Son to offer himself as a ransom for his lost children. Jesus, the beautiful Lamb who willingly sacrificed himself, did so on our behalf out of a love too great to understand. His dying thoughts were of you.

Through his blood, as he hung on the cross of Calvary, Jesus saw you standing beside his mother and the apostle that he loved. For you were predestined to be saved by grace, which is the free gift of God for every believer. For you, grace hung upon that tree,

HE SETS THE PRISONER FREE ~ SHAWN HURLEY

cursing sin in the flesh and rescuing you from the snare of death. He loved you from the very beginning, and his great sacrifice was an eternal kiss from his heart. If, therefore, you ever doubt his love, simply gaze at the cross, which is not a symbol of defeat or shame but the most amazing expression of love his children could ever experience.

Gaze at the cross as divine love pours from his eyes and his precious heart, his body broken for you. You will then readily understand why Paul so confidently asked,

> Who shall separate us from the love of Christ? Shall trouble or hardship or persecution or famine or nakedness or danger or sword? .... For I am convinced that neither death nor life, neither angels nor demons, neither the present nor the future, nor any powers, neither height nor depth, nor anything else in all creation, will be able to separate us from the love of God that is in Christ Jesus our Lord. (Romans 8:35, 38–39)

Love fulfilled the law because *he* is love—love so great that he substituted himself for every soul born of Adam. Gaze at him and weep tears of unlimited joy; sing the song of songs, because in his dying moments, he saw you free, whole, and perfect. He saw you as a new creation, and it made all his suffering worthwhile. Because he first loved you, you can love him. What incredible love! What a magnificent God!

THE VINE AND THE BRANCHES

He cried, "It is finished," and then he breathed his last. But death is never the end for those in the family of King Jesus. In that glorious moment, it all came together. "I will not leave you as orphans; I will come to you" (John 14:18). These words melted the hearts of his disciples. This was the promise of one who laid down his life for his friends. "I will ask the Father, and he will give you another Helper, to be with you forever." The Son dies so that the Spirit might live in each child of the Father.

He asks only that we keep his commandments, for that is the testimony of our love for him. The beloved disciple goes so far as to write, "We know that we have come to know him if we keep his commands" (1 John 2:3). When we keep his commandments, we have come to know him, for whoever keeps them, the love of God is truly perfected in him. And what are those commandments? "And this is his command: to believe in the name of his Son, Jesus Christ, and to love one another as he commanded us" (1 John 3:23). "No one has ever seen God; but if we love one another, God lives in us and his love is made complete in us" (1 John 4:12).

Love is the key to knowing him and proof that his love has been perfected in us. But we come to that love, not by striving or working but simply by gazing upon our beautiful Lord, receiving his love, and loving him in return. "Jesus replied, 'Anyone who loves me will obey my teaching. My Father will love them, and we will come to them and make our home with them'" (John 14:23). When we love the slain Lamb and all those for whom he died, the Father, Son, and Holy Spirit come and make their home with us.

HE SETS THE PRISONER FREE ~ SHAWN HURLEY

We become temples of the Holy Spirit—temples of the living God. He saw you, not as a flawed human being but as a new creation in Christ, the new Holy of Holies. We are precious in the sight of God the Father. Much more, we are branches intrinsically rooted to the vine, for in him we live and move and have our being. Two were made one in a bond of perfection called love.

We become love, not by our own efforts or by endlessly striving but simply by abiding in him, gazing at him, and allowing him to become one with each one of us. Those who yearn for fruit in their Christian walk often struggle and strain to produce it, but Christ did not intend this. In coming to take up his home in you, he sought to work through you. All you have to do is yield and be an open vessel through whom he can manifest.

Becoming love is the fruit of the vine. If we are the branches, then it is not our job to force out fruit or struggle to produce it. As one with the vine, we simply produce fruit without effort or strain. The apple tree produces apples, not by willpower but because that is what it is: a tree that produces apples. Likewise, we become love because, thanks to the finished work of the cross, we are connected to the root source of love. We manifest miracles because they, too, are the fruit of love.

The branch rests in the vine; it draws all it needs to survive from this source of life. As new creations in Christ, we enjoy the privilege of that same type of union with our Father. The energy of the vine lives in and through the branches and flows through us. We bear fruit only because we have been grafted into the vine, but

THE VINE AND THE BRANCHES

a branch that does not abide in the vine simply withers and falls away. Fulfilling our union with him means abiding in him so that we partake of his full and perfect nature.

If we are one with him, we do not need to beg him to come to us. That is an Old Testament mindset. We have been fully reconciled to Abba through the precious blood of his Son. Hence, he is always in us and with us because "Christ is all, and is in all" (Colossians 3:11). We do not enjoy his presence based on how we feel or behave. His presence never leaves because the kingdom of heaven is inside us.

So much of what we call prayer is predicated on a belief that we are still somehow separated from God. However, if Christ destroyed the sin that separated us from the Father, then why do we continue to pray as though we are still struggling with sin instead of seeing that we have become the righteousness of God in Christ Jesus? If in him, we live and move and have our being, then separation is a deception. In other words, how can Christ be in me—the hope of glory—and yet be separated from me at the same time? What took place on the cross canceled all previous division.

That is why the question of our identity in Christ is so crucial, for only when we know and accept that we are fully in him will we have the confidence to abide. The extraordinary words from Ephesians reveal the divine union that Christ purchased for us through the cross:

HE SETS THE PRISONER FREE ~ SHAWN HURLEY

> But now in Christ Jesus you who once were far off have been brought near by the blood of Christ. For He himself is our peace, who has made us both one and has broken down in His flesh the dividing wall of hostility by abolishing the law of commandments expressed in ordinances, that He might create in himself one new man in place of the two, so making peace, and might reconcile us both to God in one body through the cross, thereby killing the hostility. And He came and preached peace to you who were far off and peace to those who were near. For through Him we both have access in one Spirit to the Father. So then you are no longer strangers and aliens, but you are fellow citizens with the saints and members of the household of God, built on the foundation of the apostles and prophets, Christ Jesus Himself being the cornerstone, in whom the whole structure, being joined together, grows into a holy temple in the Lord. In Him you also are being built together into a dwelling place for God by the Spirit. (Ephesians 2:13–22)

In other words, prayer in its highest form is not shouting to the skies but a matter of becoming still in his presence to enjoy our divine union with him. Because he lives in you as his dwelling place, he already knows all about you and your needs. As we rest in Christ, we effortlessly produce the fruit of the Spirit. This means that prayer *is* intimacy; it is acknowledging the reality of our union

THE VINE AND THE BRANCHES

with him. In acknowledging that union, we rest in him, we abide in love, and we become love.

"Be still, and know that I am God" (Psalm 46:10 NKJV). Being still in the sacred silence is an act of faith in the presence of the Father. You sit in oneness with him, abiding in his love and allowing him to minister to you as he pleases. This is what it means to surrender; you trust that in the divine presence, he will do whatever is necessary for your highest good. Remember, our God is pure perfection, so what he does in the silence cannot be anything less than perfect. In the silence of abiding, we do not come with a list of demands simply because we trust that our Father already knows all our needs (Matthew 6:32). Rather, in seeking first the kingdom, all those things will be added to us, for it is the Father's good pleasure to give us the kingdom (Matthew 6:33).

We sit in the holy silence, enjoying the presence of our Savior. In doing so, we turn to where Christ is in me, and the first manifestation of his presence is that peace which surpasses all understanding. Too often, we think of peace as simply the absence of strife or division. However, when Jesus speaks of peace, he uses the Hebraic word *shalom*. Shalom means much more than the absence of conflict or division; it means wholeness, well-being, abundance, completeness, soundness, and salvation.[1] Therefore,

---

[1] *Strong's Concordance*, "7965. Shalom," Bible Hub, accessed February 11, 2023, https://biblehub.com/hebrew/7965.htm.

HE SETS THE PRISONER FREE ~ SHAWN HURLEY

when Jesus says, "Peace I leave with you; my peace I give you. I do not give to you as the world gives. Do not let your hearts be troubled and do not be afraid" (John 14:27), he is declaring perfect health, wholeness, and abundance over all who have ears to hear. What we experience in the deep silence is, thus, *the shalom of Christ*—his wholeness, perfection, and abundance.

Resting in him is the key to wholeness of body, mind, and spirit. We rest in the arms of love, and in that sacred union, we are healed because Christ *is* health—he is our healer. Living in divine health requires that we surrender to him in the silence so that his power, love, and perfection can flow through us as divine life.

We close our eyes and sit still. We breathe slowly and deeply. We are not waiting for God to show up, but rather, we accept that he lives in us and is already here. The mind may initially resist the silence of God's presence, but the purpose of abiding is to spend time with your first love by surrendering to his loving embrace. His presence remains with us. The union purchased on the cross cannot ever change; we are always one with him, and the purpose of being with him in the silence is simply to enjoy that union in all its fulness.

Eventually, the chattering mind will be still, and in that stillness, we experience the great mystery of Christ in us. Because we possess the mind of Christ (1 Corinthians 2:16), we begin to think like him and hear him and become open to the inner promptings of the Spirit. Most especially, we begin to love like him

THE VINE AND THE BRANCHES

and to manifest that love in compassion and healing. The fruit of righteousness and sonship is nurtured in intimacy.

My quest to become a Franciscan monk at the age of nineteen was primarily driven by a deep yearning to savor the presence of God in silent contemplation. Even at that tender age, I read all the great masters of the contemplative tradition: saints and mystics like Augustine, Catherine of Sienna, Teresa of Avila, John of the Cross, Meister Eckhart, and, most especially, the Trappist monk Thomas Merton. Interestingly, all these contemplatives were Catholic. The old church had a long history of pursuing the presence through silent praise and devotion. As early as the year 270 AD, Christian mystics living in Egypt moved to the desert to live a life of silence and denial. Soon after, an entire community formed around them, one of which we know today as the Desert Fathers. They exerted enormous influence over the development of early Christianity, and their influence can be seen throughout church history. Indeed, the model for all churches on "practicing the presence of God" is that of the sixteenth-century Dominican friar, Brother Lawrence, whose little book of that name is a universally loved, classic devotional.

I devoured Eckhart and Merton because they gave me a new vision of how to see and experience God. Eckhart wrote that "there is nothing more like God than silence," whereas Merton said that "in silence God ceases to be an object and becomes an

HE SETS THE PRISONER FREE ~ SHAWN HURLEY

experience."[2] He becomes an experience because in the silence, you abandon all your preconceptions of the Father—all those images and misrepresentations that culture and bad theology have taught to you from childhood. You now experience him as he is: the great I Am—pure, unconditional love.

I was the prodigal son seeking a way home to my father, and in that journey, I dropped all resistance and let him love me as only Father God can. I came to know his heart in those moments of silence. When you immerse yourself in the Father's divine life and love in silent contemplation, you can hear him speak. Otherwise, you will drown out his voice with your own as you petition and pray. Indeed, simply by entering that union, you receive all that the Father wants to lavish upon you.

"But when you pray, go into your room, close the door and pray to your Father, who is unseen. Then your Father, who sees what is done in secret, will reward you" (Matthew 6:6). Obviously, those whom Jesus was addressing had, if they were lucky, only a single room in which to live. So he was talking about the inner room of the heart, where the Father dwells. (The kingdom of heaven is *within*.) In this place of divine union, Abba reveals the secrets of the kingdom. You enter with the faith of a little child, and then you hear those life-transforming words: "All that I have is

---

[2] Friends of Silence, Home, accessed February 10, 2023, https://friendsofsilence.net/quote/1994/10/nothing-so-much-god; Scott Johnson, "The Spirit Speaks In Silence," Wineskins, June 4, 2018, https://wineskins.org/2018/06/04/the-spirit-speaks-in-silence/.

THE VINE AND THE BRANCHES

thine." Learning to abide in the Father is learning how to be a son—one who stands to inherit the kingdom. That is why our beautiful Savior tells us to always "seek first his kingdom and his righteousness, and all these things will be given to you as well" (Matthew 6:33, emphasis added). Our relationship with Abba is the only thing we need, for out of that, "all these things will be added unto you."

We begin to experience "in the coming ages he might show the incomparable riches of his grace, expressed in his kindness to us in Christ Jesus" (Ephesians 2:7). We experience his tender affection and know that he has blessed us with every spiritual blessing in Christ (Ephesians 1:3–4). All that he has is ours because our lives are hidden with Christ, so that when he appears, we will also appear with him in glory. Does this seem too good to be true? It is simply the life of a son beloved of his heavenly Father.

HE SETS THE PRISONER FREE ~ SHAWN HURLEY

Chapter 7

GREATER WORKS THAN THESE

Much of the confusion surrounding divine healing is due to the mistaken belief that if you say the right prayer or do the right things, people will get healed. The problem with this is that it tends to reduce the glorious power of Christ to a set of techniques. Hence, when one technique fails to heal a person, another is used in the hope that it might prove more successful.

Yes, Jesus used different ways to heal, sometimes laying his hands on people, and sometimes commanding healing with a word. However, his purpose was not to equip us with techniques but simply to demonstrate the will of God for healing and to show us what life in union with him would look like. Indeed, what he modeled for us was a life lived in total intimacy with the Father, and out of that intimacy flowed the supernatural lifestyle that we are all called to live.

HE SETS THE PRISONER FREE ~ SHAWN HURLEY

I have spent time in this book discussing the key themes of identity, love, and intimacy. Put simply, healing does not happen because of a principle, a method, or a technique. Healing happens because of our identity in him and our time spent enjoying divine union. It happens because his love in you loves the person standing in front of you. It happens because he nailed sickness, death, sin, and separation to the cross. It happens because Jesus's entire ministry was devoted to healing the sick, raising the dead, cleansing lepers, and casting out demons. And now, the same Jesus that did all that and so much more lives inside you. Christ in you *is* your hope of glory.

Now that Christ lives in you, whoever has seen you has seen the Father. As Christ's representative, you are now the exact imprint of the Father's nature. As such, you, too, can say that you will do the works of the Christ who dwells in you. The staggering realization that you and the Father are one, that you are a co-heir with Christ of his kingdom, is the key to walking in healing miracles. At some point, all that I have written in this book about our divine union must become a tangible reality for you. You must wake up every morning *knowing* that you are a beloved son of God and the exact imprint of his divine nature.

We must come to a place where we fully embrace the truth that the kingdom of heaven is within us and that all that we have is his is so that we can finally accept our divine inheritance. But that will only come when intimacy is given first place in our lives. Too often, we seek power at the expense of love. We desire miracles before we get to know the Miracle Worker. We want the things of the kingdom before we see ourselves as sons of a beautiful King.

My healing ministry is not based on formulas and techniques but on obedience, surrender, and love of God and my neighbor. There are plenty of how-to healing books and even more videos available demonstrating techniques of divine healing. My aim is not to criticize these or to say that I possess a better way to access the keys of the kingdom. But Jesus promised that we could do greater things, which flow from oneness with him and the Father. That is why he prayed the following the night before he died:

> My prayer is not for them alone. I pray also for those who will believe in me through their message, that all of them may be one, Father, just as you are in me and I am in you. May they also be in us so that the world may believe that you have sent me. I have given them the glory that you gave me, that they may be one as we are one—I in them and you in me—so that they may be brought to complete unity. Then the world will know that you sent me and have loved them even as you have loved me. (John 17:20–23)

Once again, the glory that sons of God will manifest on this earth will come through unity and oneness with Christ and our Father.

A lot more emphasis needs to be placed on self-healing in supernatural ministry. Yes, we are commanded as believers to "heal

HE SETS THE PRISONER FREE ~ SHAWN HURLEY

the sick, raise the dead, cleanse the lepers and cast out demons," but what happens when the healing minister is not in town or when there is no believer to lay hands on the sick person? There is a fundamental need to emphasize that *all* healing (for self and others) flows directly out of each believer's personal union, oneness, and presence.

Christ in you is the focus of ministry, whether giving or receiving. You are, in effect, pouring divine life into the person in need so that you can minister effectively. We share the love, peace, and perfection that we receive in the silence when we fulfill the divine mandate to heal the sick.

Our beautiful Savior told us to have faith in God. Furthermore, he promised that "if anyone says to this mountain, 'Go, throw yourself into the sea,' and does not doubt in their heart but believes that what they say will happen, it will be done for them" (Mark 11:23). More astonishingly still, he assured us that "whatever you ask for in prayer, believe that you have received it, and it will be yours" (Mark 11:24). These glorious promises were made in the context of Jesus cursing a fig tree. The following morning, as Jesus and his disciples again passed by the tree, they found it withered all the way to its roots. The great lesson on healing from this incident is that when you place your hands on a sick person and speak to their mountain, you are to believe that you *have* received what you asked for, and you shall have it. Notice that Jesus says we must believe that the healing is already accomplished—*even if we do not see any immediate sign of it*. The fig tree

GREATER WORKS THAN THESE

withered away overnight, but it began to wither once Christ commanded it to do so. There should be no begging for the sick to be healed. That divine assurance that God hears us is the guarantee that faith in God is sufficient to remove any mountain.

"Now faith is confidence in what we hope for and assurance about what we do not see" (Hebrews 11:1). Faith is the currency of things that are not seen and yet are believed. Jesus did not see the fig tree wither, but he knew that it was dead once he gave the word. He brought forth the unseen from the seen through his authority. This is faith: not that something will happen but that it has already happened despite the lack of any immediate proof.

Healing happens with that type of confidence. Often, miracles will happen instantaneously, and I document many in the next chapter. However, healing can also be progressive as with the example of the fig tree. Either way, what heals the person is not what you say or how loudly you say it but rather your belief in Jesus. *We have his faith* when we believe that we have already received the faith of Jesus. Through our divine union, we have the faith, love, and hope of Christ.

Jesus destroyed the works of the devil through love. So confident was he in his union with the Father, that when he ministered, he had full confidence in the Father to do the works. We must have that same confidence because we are now the temples of the living God. We have the faith of Christ when we know that he is in us and that we are in him. And to have the faith

HE SETS THE PRISONER FREE ~ SHAWN HURLEY

of Christ is to have the love of Christ for everyone without exception.

Love the sick and you will heal the sick. Love the brokenhearted, and you will restore them to new life. Love the stranger, and you will be to him a home. Love the lost, and you will offer them the chance of salvation. Love in every trial and circumstance, and you will triumph above them all. Love and the glory of the Christ within you will cast aside all darkness. Love and you will have all the faith you need to move any mountain.

In the end, putting on love is the real secret to divine healing, which is why the only real training you need is to sit in the silence. Only in the intimacy of the secret place can we fall in love with love. In that sacred union, we partake of his divine power. And from there, we shall do the greater works for which "the whole creation has been groaning as in the pains of childbirth right up to the present time" (Romans 8:22).

Chapter 8
WALKING IN POWER

From prodigal son to a child of the Most High, I have sought to live out my Christ-given identity in simple love for every soul I encounter. In the second section of this book, I have shown you how to follow me on that path of righteousness that King Jesus purchased for us. If you live from your new-creation identity by becoming love, you shall, indeed, do the greater works that Christ promised as part of your divine inheritance. By giving his presence first place in your life, you will find that miracles become commonplace. Please believe me when I say that abiding in him is the true key to walking in signs and wonders.

In this final chapter, I want to share some testimonies of what you can do if you live from the secret place and accept your full inheritance as a coheir of the kingdom with Jesus. These miracle stories are not meant to highlight my gift as a divine healer. I do not possess any special gift. The works I do are simply an

HE SETS THE PRISONER FREE ~ SHAWN HURLEY

overflow of dwelling in love and savoring my sonship. As I have shown in this book, this is the birthright of any believer. If he abides in you and you abide in him, you, too, can undertake the heavenly tasks of healing the sick, casting out demons, and raising the dead to new life. Therefore, these stories of answered prayer should encourage you to go and do likewise. Spend time loving him and accepting his love.

My entire purpose in writing this book was to show that if I can do the miraculous, anyone can. I began with my personal testimony so that you can see that no matter how rebellious you have been, no matter how lost or broken your life seems to be, our loving Father will always be there, waiting for you. Run to him, let him clothe you in his robe of righteousness and place his gold ring upon your finger. You are his child, and he desperately wants to be your first love. He yearns to work through you so that his mercy, gentleness, and healing power can saturate your family, society, and all those who happen to pass your way.

Let me once again give you the best advice that I possess on healing and the supernatural: *Spend time in his arms*. Give him first place in your life, and everything else will follow. The kingdom of heaven is within you.

For example, when praying over objects, such as cloths, to give to people, there is a biblical basis for this found in Acts 19:12. "So that even handkerchiefs and aprons that had touched him were taken to the sick, and their illnesses were cured and the evil spirits left them." In one very special case, I sent a cloth to a mother whose unborn baby was declared dead by her doctors. She placed the cloth on her abdomen, and her child came back to life. Another lady asked me to send her a cloth because her husband was in the hospital dying of cancer. She placed the cloth on him as he slept, and she went home. Shortly after, his tests showed no trace of cancer, and he made a full recovery.

Testimonies like this are important because they demonstrate the tangible power of God in our midst. However, they are equally necessary as a way of encouraging believers to go into all the world. Once you realize that he dwells inside you, then you can freely give his love and peace to those who need it.

For example, a man once asked me to contact his son who he said was struggling. When I phoned the son, he said that he was in the hospital suffering with AIDS. I explained the gospel of salvation and the finished work of Christ to show him why his sins were forgiven. Then I asked him if he wanted to be rid of his affliction, to which he naturally agreed. In love, I commanded the demon to leave his body, and that respectful young man thanked me, and we ended the call. Soon after, his father sent me a text to say that his son no longer had AIDS. All I did in that instance was to love the boy as Christ loves him. No demon or affliction can withstand that type of love.

Forgiveness *is* love, and Jesus directly tied healing and forgiveness together. Christ's finished work was one of radical forgiveness: He reconciled us to the Father by nailing our sins to the cross. In that moment, they were completely erased as though

HE SETS THE PRISONER FREE ~ SHAWN HURLEY

they had never happened. Listen again to these glorious words from Paul: "When you were dead in your sins and in the uncircumcision of your flesh, God made you alive with Christ. He forgave us all our sins, having canceled the charge of our legal indebtedness, which stood against us and condemned us; he has taken it away, nailing it to the cross" (Colossians 2:13–14).

However, even before the cross, he demonstrated the fundamental link between healing and forgiveness. "Some men brought to him a paralyzed man, lying on a mat. When Jesus saw their faith, he said to the man, "Take heart, son; your sins are forgiven"' (Matthew 9:2). In my healing ministry, I have very often found that a refusal to forgive can somehow block a healing, or, indeed, if a person cannot receive forgiveness, this, too, can prevent healing. The paralytic's healing was predicated on divine forgiveness, and that is why, if there seems to be something standing in the way of a healing, I will ask the Holy Spirit to show me if forgiveness is an issue.

For example, one day, a couple flew me to see a young lady. As she walked, she dragged her foot, which greatly impaired her mobility. She had been receiving physical therapy, which was proving ineffective against the condition. As it happened, she was also a Spirit-filled believer in the Lord. However, as I prayed, I saw an image of a woman shouting at a little girl: "Shut up! Shut up!" I asked the lady if this meant anything, and she said that her mother used to scream this at her every time she was sick.

WALKING IN POWER

This word of knowledge built her faith for healing, but the key was to get her to forgive her mother. So, I simply said: "Let's forgive your mother. She couldn't possibly have known your God-given value as she didn't even know her own." The lady forgave her mother from her heart and, after we prayed again, she was able to walk freely.

Every day, I post numerous healing testimonies on my Facebook page, all of which happen because I surrender my life to him in the secret place. There is no other way of becoming love—of putting off the old and putting on the new, of assuming your birthright as a son of God—than by resting in him. He desires intimacy, friendship, and relationship; and he paid a high price for it.

You have been called to a glorious life, but you are not alone. "Whoever has my commands and keeps them is the one who loves me. The one who loves me will be loved by my Father, and I too will love them and show myself to them" (John 14:21).

HE SETS THE PRISONER FREE ~ SHAWN HURLEY

AFTERWORD

My primary purpose in writing this book was to show you the beautiful love and mercy of our incredible God. In sharing my life story, I wanted to demonstrate how readily salvation is available for even the worst sinner. As you have seen, I was lost and rebellious and, to the natural eye, totally beyond redemption. However, as a lost sheep, I was not forsaken by the one who loves us. My salvation was instant, but it was also a long process of learning how to walk out the Christian life. The new creation life is one of becoming more like Christ.

> For this reason I kneel before the Father, from whom every family[a] in heaven and on earth derives its name. I pray that out of his glorious riches he may strengthen you with power through his Spirit in your inner being, so that Christ may dwell in your hearts through faith. And I pray that you, being rooted and established in love, may have power, together with all the Lord's holy people, to grasp how wide

HE SETS THE PRISONER FREE ~ SHAWN HURLEY

and long and high and deep is the love of Christ, and to know this love that surpasses knowledge—that you may be filled to the measure of all the fullness of God. (Ephesians 3:14–19)

ABOUT THE AUTHOR

Shawn Hurley is an internationally admired healing evangelist. He travels the world, ministering healing to the sick, raising the dead, and casting out demons. Yet it wasn't always that way. For most of his life, he was in trouble with the law, a drug addict, homeless, and a man intent on causing pain to the people he claimed to love.

Then, one day while sitting in a jail cell, he was consumed by the unquenchable fire of God's unconditional love. Thus began a radical transformation from serial convict to crusader for Christ.

In Part 1 of this candid yet profound book, Shawn shares his astonishing testimony of how he moved from prodigal son to a saint saved by grace. In Part 2, he takes the reader on a journey into the heart of divine intimacy. Through a series of simple and beautiful teachings, he shows that all believers can do the greater things of God if they live in love and walk in the peace of Christ.

He Sets the Prisoner Free is both the remarkable story of a renowned Christian healer who has given new life and hope to thousands of people across the globe and an inspirational roadmap to show how you can follow in his footsteps.

HE SETS THE PRISONER FREE ~ SHAWN HURLEY

www.ingramcontent.com/pod-product-compliance
Lightning Source LLC
Chambersburg PA
CBHW070201100426
42743CB00013B/3000